DISTRIBUTED PROGRAMMING WITH RUBY

Mark Bates

Addison-Wesley

Upper Saddle River, NJ • Boston • Indianapolis • San Francisco
New York • Toronto • Montreal • London • Munich • Paris • Madrid
Capetown • Sydney • Tokyo • Singapore • Mexico City

Many of the designations used by manufacturers and sellers to distinguish their products are claimed as trademarks. Where those designations appear in this book, and the publisher was aware of a trademark claim, the designations have been printed with initial capital letters or in all capitals.

The author and publisher have taken care in the preparation of this book, but make no expressed or implied warranty of any kind and assume no responsibility for errors or omissions. No liability is assumed for incidental or consequential damages in connection with or arising out of the use of the information or programs contained herein.

The publisher offers excellent discounts on this book when ordered in quantity for bulk purchases or special sales, which may include electronic versions and/or custom covers and content particular to your business, training goals, marketing focus, and branding interests. For more information, please contact:

> U.S. Corporate and Government Sales
> 800-382-3419
> corpsales@pearsontechgroup.com

For sales outside the United States, please contact:

> International Sales
> international@pearson.com

Visit us on the web: informit.com/ph

Library of Congress Cataloging-in-Publication Data:

Bates, Mark, 1976-
   Distributed programming with Ruby / Mark Bates.
      p. cm.
   Includes bibliographical references and index.
   ISBN 978-0-321-63836-6 (pbk. : alk. paper) 1. Ruby (Computer program language)
2. Electronic data processing—Distributed processing. 3. Object-oriented methods
(Computer science) I. Title.
   QA76.73.R83B38 2010
   005.1'17—dc22

                                                         2009034095

ISBN-13: 978-0-321-63836-6
ISBN-10: 0-321-63836-0
Text printed in the United States on recycled paper at RR Donnelley and Sons in Crawfordsville, Indiana
First printing November 2009

Editor-in-Chief
Mark Taub

Acquisitions Editor
Debra Williams Cauley

Development Editor
Songlin Qiu

Managing Editor
Kristy Hart

Senior Project Editor
Lori Lyons

Copy Editor
Gayle Johnson

Indexer
Brad Herriman

Proofreader
Apostrophe Editing Services

Publishing Coordinator
Kim Boedigheimer

Cover Designer
Chuti Prasertsith

Compositor
Nonie Ratcliff

To Rachel, Dylan, and Leo.
Thanks for letting Daddy hide away until the wee hours of the morning
and be absent most weekends. I love you both so very much,
and I couldn't have done this without the three of you.

Contents

Foreword

Mark's career in programming parallels mine to a certain degree. We both started developing web applications in 1996 and both did hard time in the Java world before discovering Ruby and Rails in 2005, and never looking back.

At RubyConf 2008 in Orlando, I toasted Mark on his successful talk as we sipped Piña Coladas and enjoyed the "fourth track" of that conference—the lazy river and hot tub. The topic of our conversation? Adding a title to the Professional Ruby Series in which Mark would draw from his experience building Mack, a distributed web framework, as well as his long career doing distributed programming. But most important, he would let his enthusiasm for the potentially dry subject draw in the reader while being educational. I sensed a winner, but not only as far at finding the right author. The timing was right, too.

Rails developers around the world are progressing steadily beyond basic web programming as they take on large, complex systems that traditionally would be done on Java or Microsoft platforms. As a system grows in scale and complexity, one of the first things you need to do is to break it into smaller, manageable chunks. Hence all the interest in web services. Your initial effort might involve cron jobs and batch processing. Or you might implement some sort of distributed job framework, before finally going with a full-blown messaging solution.

Of course, you don't want to reinvent anything you don't need to, but Ruby's distributed programming landscape can be confusing. In the foreground is Ruby's DRb technology, part of the standard library and relatively straightforward to use—especially for those of us familiar with parallel technologies in other languages, such as Java's RMI. But does that approach scale? And is it reliable? If DRb is not suitable for your production use, what is? If we cast our view further along the landscape, we might ask: "What about newer technologies like AMQP and Rabbit MQ? And how do we tie it all together with Rails in ways that make sense?"

Mark answers all those questions in this book. He starts with some of the deepest documentation on DRb and Rinda that anyone has ever read. He then follows with coverage of the various Ruby libraries that depend on those building blocks, always keeping in mind the practical applications of all of them. He covers assembling cloud-based servers to handle background processing, one of today's hottest topics in systems architecture. Finally, he covers the Rails-specific libraries BackgrounDRb and Delayed Job and teaches you when and how to use each.

Ultimately, one of my most pleasant surprises and one of the reasons that I think Mark is an up-and-coming superstar of the Ruby community is the hard work, productivity, and fastidiousness that he demonstrated while writing this book. Over the course of the spring and summer of this year, Mark delivered chapters and revisions week after week with clockwork regularity. All with the utmost attention to detail and quality. All packed with knowledge. And most important, all packed with strong doses of his winning personality. It is my honor to present to you the latest addition to our series, *Distributed Programming with Ruby*.

Obie Fernandez, Series Editor
September 30, 2009

Preface

I first found a need for distributed programming back in 2001. I was looking for a way to increase the performance of an application I was working on. The project was a web-based email client, and I was struggling with a few performance issues. I wanted to keep the email engine separate from the client front end. That way, I could have a beefier box handle all the processing of the incoming email and have a farm of smaller application servers handling the front end of it. That seems pretty easy and straightforward, doesn't it? Well, the language I was using at the time was Java, and the distributed interface was RMI (remote method invocation). Easy and straightforward are not words I would use to describe my experiences with RMI.

Years later I was working on a completely different project, but I had a not-too-dissimilar problem—performance. The application this time was a large user-generated content site built using Ruby on Rails. When a user wrote, edited, or deleted an article for the site, it needed to be indexed by our search engine, our site map needed to be rebuilt, and the article needed to be injected into the top of our rating engine system. As you can imagine, none of this was quick and simple. You can also probably guess that our CEO wanted all of this to happen as close to real time as possible, but without the end user's having to wait for everything to get done. To further complicate matters, we had limited system resources and millions of articles that needed to be processed.

I didn't want to burden our already-overworked applications server boxes with these tasks, so I had to offload the processing to another machine. The question came to be how I could best offload this work. The first idea was to use the database as the transfer mechanism. I could store all the information in the database that these systems would need. Then the machine that was to do the processing could poll the database at a regular interval, find any pending tasks, pull them out of the database, create the same heavy objects I already had, and then start processing them. The problem, as you most likely already know, is that I'm now placing more load on the database. I would be polling it continually, regardless of whether it contained any tasks. If it did have tasks, I would have to pull those records out of the database and use more system resources transforming the records back into those same heavy Ruby objects I already had.

What I really wanted to do was just send the fully formed Ruby objects I had already created to the other machine and let it do the processing. This would lessen the burden all around. In addition to the lighter load on the database, memory, and system resources, the machine doing the processing would work only when it was told to, and it wouldn't waste recourses by continually polling the database. Plus, without polling, the parts of the application the CEO wanted updated in near real time would get updated faster.

After I realized that what I wanted to do was to use some sort of distributed mechanism, that's when I decided to see what sort of RMI-esque features Ruby had. I was already impressed with Ruby for being a terse language, but when I found the DRb (Distributed Ruby, also known as dRuby) package, I became a believer. I found that writing distributed applications in Ruby could be simple, and dare I say fun.

Who Is This Book For?

This book is quite simply written for the intermediate to advanced Ruby developer who wants to start developing distributed applications. This book assumes that you have good knowledge of Ruby, at least at the intermediate developer level. Although we will touch on some parts of the Ruby language—particularly those that might be confusing when dealing with distributed applications—we will not be going into the language in depth.

Although you should know Ruby, this book assumes that you probably do not understand distributed programming and that this is your first venture into this world. If you have done distributed programming before, this book will help you quickly understand how to do it in Ruby. If you haven't, this book will help you understand what distributed programming is and isn't.

How Is This Book Organized?

This book is split into four parts. Part I examines what ships with the standard library in Ruby 1.8.x and beyond. We look, in depth, at understanding how DRb (dRuby or Distributed Ruby) and Rinda work. We will build some simple applications in a variety of ways and use those examples to talk about the libraries. We examine the pros and cons of DRb and Rinda. By the end of Part I, "Standard Library," you should feel comfortable and ready to build your distributed applications using these libraries.

Part II, "Third-Party Frameworks and Libraries," looks at a variety of third-party tools, libraries, and frameworks designed to make distributed programming in Ruby easy, fun, and robust. Some of these libraries build on the DRb and Rinda libraries we learned about in Part I, and others don't. Some are based on executing arbitrary code on another machine. Others are based on running code in the background to elevate performance.

Part III, "Distributed Message Queues," takes a close look at some of the leading distributed message queues available to the Ruby community. These queues can help facilitate communication and tasks between your applications. Distributed message queues can help increase your applications' performance by queuing up work to be done at a later date instead of at runtime.

Finally, Part IV, "Distributed Programming with Ruby on Rails," looks at a few libraries that are designed to work exclusively with the Ruby on Rails web framework. These libraries might already be familiar to you if you have been using Ruby on Rails for several years. But there is always something to be learned, and that's what the chapters in this part of this book will help you with.

During the course of the book, we will examine a breadth of different technologies; however, this book is not necessarily a how-to guide. Instead, you will use these different technologies to help understand the complex problems associated with distributed programming and several different ways you can solve these problems. You'll use these technologies to learn about RMI, message queues, and MapReduce, among others.

How to Run the Examples

I have tried to make this book as easy to use and follow as possible. When a new technology is referenced or introduced, I give you a link to find out more about it and/or its developer(s). When you see a code sample, unless otherwise stated, I present that sample in its entirety. I have also taken extra effort to make sure that you can easily run each of those code samples as is. Unless otherwise stated, you should be able to take any code sample, copy it into a Ruby file, and run it using the `ruby` command, like this:

```
$ ruby foo.rb
```

There are times when a file needs to be named something specific or has to be run with a special command. In particular, Chapter 4, "Starfish," covers this issue. At that time I will call your attention to these details so that you can run the examples without hassle.

In some chapters, such as Chapters 2, "Rinda," and 8, "AMQP/RabbitMQ," background servers need to be run for the examples to run correctly. It is highly recommended that you restart these background servers between each set of examples that are presented in these chapters. A lot of these chapters iteratively build on a piece of software, and restarting the servers between runs helps eliminate potentially confusing results.

Acknowledgments

Writing a book isn't easy. I know that's an obvious statement, but sometimes I think people just don't quite get what goes into writing a book. I didn't think it would be this difficult. Thankfully, though, I have somehow made it out the other side. I'm a little (more like a lot) battered, bruised, and very tired, but it was definitely worth it.

However, I couldn't have done this without a lot of help from a lot of different people. As with a good Oscar speech, I'll try to keep this brief, and I'm sure, as with an Oscar speech, I'll leave out some people. If I've left you out, I apologize. Now, let's see if I can get through this before the orchestra plays me off.

First, and foremost, I have to thank my family. Rachel, my beautiful wife, has been so supportive and understanding, not just with this book, but with everything I do. I know that she would've loved to have had me spend my weekend afternoons going for walks with her. Or to have me do the stuff around the house that needs to get done. Instead, she let me hide away in my office/studio, diligently (sometimes) working on my book. The same goes for Dylan, my son. I'm sure he would've preferred to have Daddy playing with him all day. I'm all yours now, little buddy. And to little Leo: This book and you share a very similar timeline—only two days separate your birth and this book going to print. Welcome, son! Your mother and big brother will tell you this hasn't been easy, and you're better for having slept through the whole thing.

Before I get off the subject of family, I would like to thank my parents. The reasons are obvious. They brought me into this world. (And, from what I've been told, they can take me out as well.) They have always supported me and have made me the man I am today. Because of them I am not afraid to take risks. I'm not afraid to fail. In general, I'm not afraid. Except for dogs. I'm afraid of dogs, but I don't think that's my parents' fault.

I would also like to quickly thank the rest of my friends, family, and coworkers. Mostly I'm thanking them for not telling me to shut up whenever I started talking about my book, which, let me tell you, was a lot. Even I got tired of hearing about it!

In November 2008, I gave a presentation titled "Building Distributed Applications" at RubyConf in Florida. After my presentation I was approached by a couple of gentlemen telling me how much they enjoyed my talk. They wanted to know where they could find out more about DRb and Rinda. I told them that unfortunately very little documentation on the subject existed—just a few blog posts here and there, and the code itself. They told me I should write a book about distributed programming with Ruby, adding that they would order it in a heartbeat. I thought it was a great idea. Shortly before I sent my manuscript to the publisher, I received an email from one of these gentlemen, Ali Rizvi. He had stumbled across one of my blog posts on a completely unrelated subject (the iPhone), and he realized who I was and that I was writing this book. He dropped me a quick note to say hi and that he was looking forward to reading the book. So Ali, now that I know your name, thank you for the idea!

At that same conference I found myself having a few drinks in the hot tub with none other than Obie Fernandez, the Professional Ruby Series editor for Addison-Wesley. He told me how much he enjoyed my presentation earlier that day. I used the opportunity to pitch him my book idea—the one I'd had only an hour before. He loved the idea and told me he thought it would be a great book, and he would love to be a part of it. A few weeks later I received an email from Debra Williams Cauley at Addison-Wesley, wanting to talk to me about the book. The rest, as they say, is history.

Obie and Debra have been my guiding light with this book. Obie has given me great advice and guidance on writing it. His direction as a series editor has been invaluable. Thank you, Obie, for your mentoring, and thank you for helping me get this opportunity.

Debra, thank you. Thank you so much. Debra managed this book. She answered all my questions (some good, some bad); she was always there with an answer. She never told me a request was too outrageous. She helped guide me through the treacherous waters of book writing, and it's because of her that I managed to make it through to the other end mostly unscathed. I can't say enough great things about Debra, and I know I can never thank her as much as she deserves to be thanked in regards to this book. Thank you, Debra.

I would like to thank Songlin Qiu. Songlin's amazing technical editing is, quite frankly, what made this book readable. She constantly kept me on my toes and made sure not only that the book was consistent, but also that it was well written and worth reading. I'm pretty sure she also fixed a million misuses of the "its" that appeared in the book. Thank you, Songlin.

Gayle Johnson also deserves a thank you here for her copy editing. She is the one who turned my words into poetry. Well, maybe poetry is an exaggeration, but trust me—this book is a lot more enjoyable to read because of her. She turned my Guinness soaked ramblings into coherent English. Thank you, Gayle.

Lori was my project editor on this book. She helped to guide me through the murky waters that are the copy editing/pre-production phase of writing a book. Thank you, Lori, for helping me take my book to the printer.

I would like to acknowledge another group of people—technical reviewers. They read the book and told me all the things they don't like about it. Just kidding—sort of. They are my peers. Their job is to read the book and give me feedback on what they liked, disliked, and were indifferent to. Their comments ranged from "Why didn't you talk about such-and-such?" to "I like how you flow from this subject to that one." Some of these people I came to absolutely love, either because they offered me great advice or because they liked what I had done. Others I came to be frustrated with, either because I didn't like their comments or because they were right, and I don't like being wrong. Either way, all the feedback was extremely helpful. So with that said, here is a list of those people, in no particular order: Gregg Pollack, Robert P.J. Day, Jennifer Lindner, and Ilya Grigorik. Thank you all so very much.

I want to thank everyone at Addison-Wesley who worked on this book. Thank you to those who dedicated their time to making my dream into a reality. I know there are people who are working hard in the background that I am unaware of, from the cover art, to the technical editing, to the page layout, to the technical reviewers, to the person who corrects my spelling, thank you.

Finally, thank *you*. Thank you for spending your time and your money on this book. I appreciate it very, very much.

About the Author

Mark Bates has been developing web applications of one kind or another since 1996. He has spent an ungodly amount of time programming Java, but thankfully he discovered Ruby in late 2005, and life has been much nicer since.

Since discovering Ruby, Mark has become a prominent member of the community. He has developed various open-source projects, such as Configatron, Cachetastic, Genosaurus, APN on Rails, and the Mack Framework, just to name a few. The Mack Framework brought Mark to the forefront of distributed programming in the Ruby community. Mack was a web framework designed from the ground up to aid in the development of distributed applications.

Mark has taught classes on both Ruby and Ruby on Rails. He has spoken at several Ruby gatherings, including 2008's RubyConf, where he spoke about building distributed applications.

Mark has an honors degree in music from the Liverpool Institute for Performing Arts. He still likes to rock out on the weekends, but set times are now 10 p.m., not 2 a.m.

He lives just outside of Boston with his wife Rachel and their son Dylan, both of whom he missed very much when writing this book.

Mark can be found at http://www.markbates.com and http://github.com/markbates.

PART I
Standard Library

The first part of this book takes a deep dive into the two main libraries that ship with the Ruby standard library that are meant for use with distributed programming. Those two libraries are DRb (often referred to as dRuby) and Rinda.

Although these libraries have been included with Ruby for many years now, they have received little or no attention (or documentation). This has led to a lot of FUD (fear, uncertainty, and doubt) about what these libraries can and cannot do, and when they are appropriate to use (if at all).

During our deep, sometimes very deep, dive into these two libraries, we will discuss the pros and cons of using the libraries, the good and bad decisions made during their architecture, and finally, how you can use them—to much success, might I add—in your programs. Don't worry; we will also talk about when you should not use these libraries. There are times that you definitely shouldn't use them, to avoid performance and security issues.

This book does not profess to be the ultimate reference material for these libraries, but it certainly is the most documentation ever assembled on DRb and Rinda, outside of the source code itself. It is my hope that this part of the book will lead you in the right direction when you're trying to architect your distributed application. I also hope it will help you steer clear of some of the pitfalls of these libraries and also help you find the gems hidden in there, too.

2

Part II looks at a handful of libraries and frameworks that are designed to either augment, improve, or just plain replace the DRb and Rinda libraries. Although it might be tempting to jump straight into those libraries, it is important that you first understand how DRb and Rinda work, because they are the underlying technologies in some of these third-party tools. Also, understanding DRb and Rinda will help you appreciate, and evaluate, these third-party libraries.

CHAPTER 1

Distributed Ruby (DRb)

The standard Ruby library ships with a package known as DRb. You will sometimes see this package referred to as dRuby. No matter what you call the package, they both mean the same thing, Distributed Ruby. DRb is an incredibly easy package to learn and use. It has the benefits of being written completely in Ruby and using core libraries. It also offers advantages such as automatic selection of object transmission (either pass by value or pass by reference), reasonable speed, and the ability to run on any operating system that runs Ruby (see Figure 1-1). DRb also allows you to write applications without a defined interface, which can make for faster development time. This can also be a disadvantage, as we'll talk about in a minute.

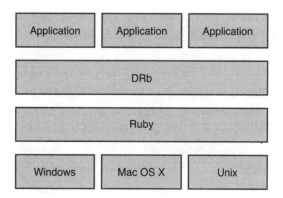

Figure 1-1   DRb can be run on any operating system capable of running Ruby.

Although DRb has its advantages, it also has disadvantages. DRb can prove to be unreliable under heavy loads. While it has reasonable speed, thanks to the underlying marshaling, socket, and thread classes, that speed can quickly degrade when placed under considerable load. Finally, DRb can tightly couple applications, because you are not calling a defined API but rather methods on objects that may or may not change over time. So although DRb might be the perfect solution for connecting a set of smaller applications, it might be unsuitable in large-scale, high-volume production environments.

With that said, it's important to discuss DRb, because it lays a nice foundation for distributed programming with Ruby, and it can definitely be useful in certain environments.

Here is what the documentation says when introducing DRb:

> *dRuby is a distributed object system for Ruby. It allows an object in one Ruby process to invoke methods on an object in another Ruby process on the same or a different machine.*

This is Ruby's equivalent of Java's RMI package. The DRb package is the basis for most of the distributed programming done in Ruby. This chapter explores the DRb package. You'll start by getting your feet wet, and by the end of the chapter you will be able to write robust, secure, and interactive applications using DRb.

Hello World

To help you get a feel for any language, framework, or package, the obligatory "Hello World" example has held up well. So why should our journey into distributed programming with Ruby be any different?

Let's start by taking a quick look at how things are done using another language's framework for distributed programming. In the introduction to this book I spoke of my past experiences using Java's RMI package, so let's use that to help us compare and contrast a bit. I promise you this will be a very brief look into the past. It will help illustrate how writing distributed applications with Ruby is quite simple.

First, when using Java RMI, we have to create an interface for our server to later implement:

```
package example.hello;

import java.rmi.Remote;
import java.rmi.RemoteException;

public interface Hello extends Remote {
  String sayHello() throws RemoteException;
}
```

We're saying that our `Hello` interface will extend the `java.rmi.Remote` class. We are also saying that any class that implements our `Hello` interface will need to provide a `sayHello` method that returns a `String`. Now that we have our interface, we can write our "Hello World" server class:

```
package example.hello;

import java.rmi.registry.Registry;
import java.rmi.registry.LocateRegistry;
import java.rmi.RemoteException;
import java.rmi.server.UnicastRemoteObject;

public class Server implements Hello {

  public Server() {}

  public String sayHello() {
    return "Hello, world!";
  }

  public static void main(String args[]) {
    try {
      Server obj = new Server();
      Hello stub = (Hello) UnicastRemoteObject.exportObject(obj, 0);

      // Bind the remote object's stub in the registry
      Registry registry = LocateRegistry.getRegistry();
      registry.bind("Hello", stub);

      System.out.println("Server ready");
    } catch (Exception e) {
```

```
    System.err.println("Server exception: " + e.toString());
    e.printStackTrace();
  }
}

}
```

In our `Server` class we are implementing our `Hello` interface. We have a `sayHello` method that returns a new `String`, `"Hello, world!"`. When we run this class, the `main` method is executed. The `main` method creates a new instance of the `Server` class. It then creates a "remoteable" stub of the `Hello` interface using the instantiated `Server` class. The `main` method then finds a `java.rmi.Registry` and binds the stub to the registry with the name `Hello`.

Before we look at the Ruby equivalent of our `Server` class, let's take a look at the Java client for our "Hello World" application:

```
package example.hello;

import java.rmi.registry.LocateRegistry;
import java.rmi.registry.Registry;

public class Client {

  private Client() {}

  public static void main(String[] args) {
    try {
      Registry registry = LocateRegistry.getRegistry();
      Hello stub = (Hello) registry.lookup("Hello");
      String response = stub.sayHello();
      System.out.println("response: " + response);
    } catch (Exception e) {
      System.err.println("Client exception: " + e.toString());
      e.printStackTrace();
    }
  }

}
```

Our client is pretty straightforward. When the class is executed, the `main` method is called. The first thing the `main` method does is find the `java.rmi.Registry`, the same registry we used in the `Server` class. Once we have access to the registry, we can call the `lookup` method and pass it the name of the service we want to use. In our case we are looking for the "Hello" service.

The `lookup` method returns to us the same stub of the `Hello` interface we bound to the registry in our `Server` class. With that stub we can call the `sayHello` method, which results in "response: Hello, world!" being printed to the screen.

That is how you would do a simple "Hello World" application using Java `RMI`. It doesn't seem that complicated or too difficult, but as you can see, there is a lot of code happening there for a just a simple "Hello World." When you start doing something more complex, you can quickly become swamped with overwhelming interfaces, classes, stubs, registries, and so on.

So how do we go about writing the Ruby/`DRb` equivalent of our Java `RMI Server` class? Well, let's take a look:

```ruby
require 'drb'

class HelloWorldServer

  def say_hello
    'Hello, world!'
  end

end

DRb.start_service("druby://127.0.0.1:61676", HelloWorldServer.new)
DRb.thread.join
```

Our `HelloWorldServer` class is pretty straightforward. In fact, only the last two lines of this example really offer anything new to a developer who is already familiar with writing Ruby applications, but let's recap quickly anyway.

First we need to require the `drb` package. We do that on the first line by calling `require 'drb'`. After that we create a simple Ruby class called `HelloWorldServer`. It's important to note that we do not have to implement any sort of interface, extend any class, or include any module. We just create our simple class with a `say_hello` method that returns the `String` `"Hello, world!"`.

With our `HelloWorldServer` class defined, we just need to bind an instance of it to a host and a port and then start the service. We do that with this line:

```ruby
DRb.start_service("druby://127.0.0.1:61676", HelloWorldServer.new)
```

Notice that we pass the start_service method an instance of the Hel-loWorldServer class and not just the constant HelloWorldServer. This is because you have to bind an instance of an object to the registry. This makes it difficult to call class-level methods using DRb. Later in the book we'll talk about, and show an example of, how to get around this small limitation. All that's left is to make sure that our server doesn't exit when the file is run:

```
DRb.thread.join
```

This prevents the Ruby virtual machine (VM) from exiting until it is forcibly quit. Otherwise, it would be a short-lived, and not very useful, server.

With our server now up and running and ready to say hello to the world, we just need a client to call it:

```
require 'drb'

server = DRbObject.new_with_uri("druby://127.0.0.1:61676")

puts server.say_hello
```

First we need to require the DRb package, just like we did with our HelloWorld-Server class. Next we need to get the instance of the HelloWorldServer class we bound when we started the server. To do that, we need to call the new_with_uri method on DRbObject. This method takes the host and port where we expect to find our HelloWorldServer class bound.

When we call DRbObject.new_with_uri("druby://127.0.0.1:61676"), we actually get back an instance of DRb::DRbObject and not the HelloWorld-Server class. Yet, on the last line of our client, we call the say_hello method on that object. If we ran it, we would see "Hello, world!" printed to the screen. So what has happened here? How did all this work? Let's start at the end and work our way back to the beginning. If we were to call inspect on the server object we received in our client, we would see something similar to this:

```
#<DRb::DRbObject:0x9cb58 @uri="druby://127.0.0.1:61676", @ref=nil>
```

DRb::DRbObject provides a wrapper around our HelloWorldServer class and provides a local stub of HelloWorldServer, similar to the stub we were returned in our Java RMI example. Using the magic of method_missing, it appears that we have an instance of HelloWorldServer. When a method is invoked on DRb::DRbObject, the method call is sent back to the remote object over the network, and the response is serialized and sent over the network connection back to the client, as shown in Figure 1-2.

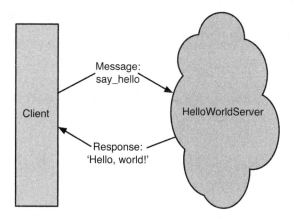

Figure 1-2   The life cycle of a standard DRb request and response.

Definition: Serialization (Marshaling)

Serialization is the process of converting an object into a series of bits that can be either stored or transmitted across a network. The process of serialization is also called marshaling. When the bits are deserialized, or unmarshaled, the original serialization format can be used to create a semantically identical clone of the original object.

To better demonstrate how method calls are sent over the network, let's quickly build a distributed logging service. Our server should serve up a Ruby Logger class and let our client send messages back to the server so that they can be written into a log, or, in our case, STDOUT.

Here is what our logging server looks like:

```
require 'drb'
require 'logger'

DRb.start_service("druby://127.0.0.1:61676", Logger.new(STDOUT))
DRb.thread.join
```

Notice that the only differences we have in our logging server example are that we call require 'logger' and are binding an instance of the Logger class to our DRb service.

Like the client application for our "Hello World" service, we just need to retrieve the stub of the instantiated Logger class from the host and port we bound it to and then invoke the method on the stub we want to call:

```
require 'drb'

logger = DRbObject.new_with_uri("druby://127.0.0.1:61676")

logger.info 'Hello, world!'
```

If we were to run our client application, we would see something like the following show up in our server logs:

```
I, [2009-02-02T23:23:38.535365 #22859]  INFO -- : Hello, world!
```

So we can see that we retrieved a reference to our remote logger in our client, called the info method, and passed it the 'Hello, world!' message. The message was received by the server and logged appropriately.

In Summary

With our "Hello World" and "Distributed Logger" applications, you have quickly started writing your first distributed applications, and you have seen how back-and-forth communication works between the server and the client. You have been introduced to the basic concepts of distributed programming and have gained a basic understanding of what the DRb package does and how it works.

Proprietary Ruby Objects

In the preceding section you got your hands dirty with a quick and simple "Hello World" application and a functional, albeit limited, "Distributed Logger." Now that you have a basic understanding of how to write simple distributed applications using DRb, let's step it up a notch and build something a bit more complex.

For our next example we will build a server that serves up a "database" of users. We want to be able to find a user by his ID, update his username, and "save" the results back to the "database." Because this isn't a book about databases, we will cheat a bit here and there, and pretend we are writing to a database. So don't worry. No SQL queries will be left hanging.

The first thing we need, even before we write our UserServer class, is a User class:

```ruby
class User

  attr_accessor :id
  attr_accessor :username

  def save
    "Saved: <#{self.id}: username: #{self.username}>"
  end

end
```

The User class is a plain Ruby object that has two accessors, id and username. We have also written a save method. This method doesn't do much but return a String saying that it saved the record. It also contains some information about the User. Again, because we are not actually writing to a database, this method should be sufficient for our needs.

With our User class defined, we can now write our UserServer class:

```ruby
require 'drb'
require 'user'

class UserServer

  attr_accessor :users

  def initialize
    self.users = []
    5.times do |i|
      user = User.new
      user.id = i + 1
      user.username = "user#{i+1}"
      self.users << user
```

```
      end
    end

    def find(id)
      self.users[id - 1]
    end

  end

  DRb.start_service("druby://127.0.0.1:61676", UserServer.new)
  DRb.thread.join
```

As will soon become a commonplace task for you, we need to require the DRb
libraries with the `require 'drb'` line that starts our script. Next we call `require
'user'` to require the User class we have written. As I mentioned earlier, this book is
about distributed programming and not databases, so we will simply mock out a database for our UserServer by creating an accessor called users. In our initialize
method we will prefill that accessor with an Array of simple User objects. We'll create five User objects with IDs of 1 to 5 and usernames of user1 to user5.

Our find method is quite simple and straightforward. It takes an id parameter
from which we subtract 1 (don't forget that our IDs start at 1 but Array indexes start
at 0) and retrieves the User object at that index in the Array.

Finally, we close our UserServer script by binding a new instance of the
UserServer at the DRb service on host 127.0.0.1 and port 61676 and join the DRb
Thread so that the application doesn't exit immediately. The UserServer class
should now be ready to fulfill the requirements we set out earlier.

Now that we have this wonderful UserServer service, we need to write a client
that uses the service. When we described the outline for this project earlier, we said
that we would need to look up a User by its id, update the username of that User,
and finally, persist the User back to the server. Let's write our client to do just that:

```
  require 'drb'

  user_server = DRbObject.new_with_uri("druby://127.0.0.1:61676")

  user = user_server.find(1)

  puts "user: #{user.inspect}"
```

```
puts "original username: #{user.username}"

user.username = 'bobsmith'

puts user.save

user = user_server.find(1)

puts "username now: #{user.username}"
```

First we need to retrieve the `UserServer` by finding it at the host and port we bound it to earlier. We accomplish this with the line `user_server = DRbObject.new_with_uri("druby://127.0.0.1:61676")`. Once we have access to the `UserServer`, we can find the `User` with the id of 1, `user = user_server.find(1)`. Out of curiosity, let's print the `inspect` on the `User` object we get from the `UserServer` to see what is returned. Next we print the `username` of the `User`, and we set the `username` of the `User` to be `'bobsmith'`. After we have updated the `username`, we need to persist the `User` object back to the `UserServer`, so we call the `save` method. Finally, just to confirm that the `username` has truly been saved, we retrieve the `User` again from the `UserServer` and print its `username` one last time.

With both our server and client written, we can finally try out our code and make sure that it all works. First we need to fire up the `UserServer`. When that is up and running, we can run our client against it. What happens when you run the client against the `UserServer` code we wrote? Well, you should get an error that looks something like this:

```
user: #<DRb::DRbUnknown:0x81e0c
@buf="\004\bo:\tUser\a:\016@username\"\nuser3:\b@idi\b", @name="User">
NoMethodError: undefined method 'username' for
#<DRb::DRbUnknown:0x81e0c>
at top level in client.rb at line 9
```

Why are we getting a `NoMethodError` on what should be a `User` object being served by the `UserServer`? In the "Distributed Logger" application we could call methods such as `info` on the `Logger` class, and that worked just fine. What's so different about the `User` class and its `username` method? Why does this `inspect` on what should be a `User` object say that it is a class of type `DRb::DRbUnknown`? In our "Hello World" application when we called the `inspect` method on the object returned over DRb, we got a class type of DRb::Object, and now we are getting a class type of DRb::DRbUnknown. These are all great questions, so why don't we address them?

> ## Definitions: Pass by Value and Pass by Reference
>
> When discussing distributed programming, the phrases *pass by value* and *pass by reference* are used often. When an object is described as being passed by value, this means that the object itself has been serialized and passed down to the client, where it will be deserialized and executed locally. When an object is described as being passed by reference, this means that an identifier is passed down to the client that references the original object back on the server. When a message is sent to the referenced object, the message is then sent back to the server, where the message is then executed against the original object.

All of the preceding questions have the same answer. When we created our "Hello World" and "Distributed Logger" applications, we were only passing Ruby objects across the wire that were part of the standard Ruby library and were not proprietary classes. DRb, when trying to figure out which method of transmission to use—pass by value or pass by reference—attempts to serialize the object in question. If the object can be serialized, as is the case with our String in the "Hello World" application, the object is serialized and sent to the client, where it can be executed locally. In our "User Server" example, the User class can be serialized, but it can't be deserialized in the client, because the client does not have the class definition for User in its virtual machine. That's why the inspect on the User class comes back with DRb::DRbUnknown and you get a NoMethodError when you try to call the username method on the returned class. How do we solve this problem? We could, of course, copy the User class definition from the UserServer to the client. That would work. The problem with this approach is that it starts to get unwieldy after a while, depending on the size of your application. Plus, you are duplicating code and generally confusing the issue.

Luckily, DRb comes with a simple built-in way of making all these problems go away. All we need to do is update our User class to look something like this:

```ruby
class User
  include DRbUndumped

  attr_accessor :id
  attr_accessor :username

  def save
    "Saved: <#{self.id}: username: #{self.username}>"
  end

end
```

The all-important line, and the only one we have added, is include DRbUn-dumped. Normally when an object is returned by a method called over DRb, the object is marshaled, sent over the connection, and run on the client side. As mentioned earlier, this works wonderfully if the object returned has a class definition that exists on the client side. When we include DRbUndumped into a class, as we did with the User class, we tell DRb that the object cannot be marshaled and that DRb should send a reference to it instead. The object then stays on the server side, and the reference on the client side then proxies the method calls back and forth to the server (see Figure 1-3). If we were to run our client now, we would expect to get output that looks something like this:

```
user: #<DRb::DRbObject:0x81ed4 @uri="druby://127.0.0.1:61676",
@ref=265930>
original username: user3
Saved: <3: username: bobsmith>
username now: bobsmith
```

Ah, success! That's more like it. We now can print the original username, update it to a different username, persist it back to the UserServer, and finally retrieve the User one last time to make sure we have actually updated the username to bobsmith.

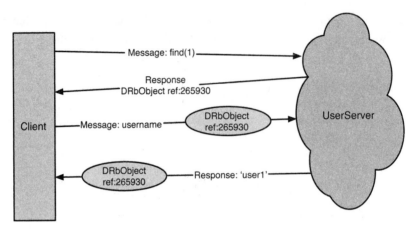

Figure 1-3   The life cycle of an average DRb pass by reference request.

I mentioned that when you include DRbUndumped, a reference to the object is sent across DRb, and not actually the object itself. If we examine the inspect from our "Hello World" application that we saw earlier and the inspect from the User object we just printed, we notice something interesting:

```
#<DRb::DRbObject:0x9cb58 @uri="druby://127.0.0.1:61676", @ref=nil>
#<DRb::DRbObject:0x81ed4 @uri="druby://127.0.0.1:61676", @ref=265930>
```

The first line is from the "Hello World" example, and the second is from the User class. You can see that for the "Hello World" inspect, it says that the @ref instance variable is nil. But for the User object it has a @ref instance variable set to the value 265930, which is the reference ID of the User object living on the server. See Figure 1-3.

In Summary

In this section we started to dig a little deeper into the innards of DRb. We built a more complex application that had proprietary Ruby objects and made use of the DRbUndumped module. We also learned how DRb decides which transmission mechanism it should use, pass by value or pass by reference. As you build your own distributed applications using DRb, you will find that the DRbUndumped module is very powerful and is the real secret sauce in making writing distributed applications with Ruby incredibly easy.

> **Fun Fact**
>
> The DRbUndumped module is actually only one method.
> That one method contains only one line of code. That one
> line of code does nothing but raise an error!
>
> ```
> module DRbUndumped
>   def _dump(dummy)   # :nodoc:
>     raise TypeError, 'can\'t dump'
>   end
> end
> ```
>
> When that error is raised, it tells DRb to reference the
> object instead of marshaling it. Because of that one line, we
> can create complex applications using proprietary objects,
> and we don't have to worry about the end user not having
> access to objects.

Security

Every developer needs to concern herself with the security of her application. With
distributed applications that security is even more of a concern and even more difficult to maintain. Although the DRb package, and Ruby, provide some security, they
fall short of a full, comprehensive solution. This can make DRb less than desirable in
a lot of real world situations. However, in situations where security is a lesser concern,
such as prototyping and intranet applications, the security that is provided with DRb
and Ruby might just suffice.

Earlier I talked about how easy it is to execute code on a remote server from the
client. This enormous security hole should have jumped right off the page at you. Let's
look at an example from the DRb RDoc (an application that produces documentation
for Ruby code):

```ruby
require 'drb'
# !!! UNSAFE CODE DO NOT RUN !!!
ro = DRbObject::new_with_uri("druby://your.server.com:8989")
class << ro
  undef :instance_eval
end
ro.instance_eval("`rm -rf *`")
```

What is this sample code doing, and why is it so dangerous? Let's examine it. First, we retrieve a new remote object from the server. Then we undefine the `instance_eval` method on that remote object. Because of how DRb works, as we learned earlier, when a method does not exist on the local copy of the remote object, the method is invoked on the server side. So in the last line, when we call the `instance_eval` method and tell it to evaluate String "\`rm -rf *\`", we are telling the remote server to forcibly, and recursively, remove all files on the server. Probably not the best idea.

How do we prevent this from happening? It's best to run your "server" code with a safe mode of at least 1: `$SAFE = 1`. This disables `eval()` and related calls on strings passed across the wire. Now, if you were to run our malicious client again, you would get the following error:

```
SecurityError: Insecure operation - instance_eval
```

Setting your safe level to 1 will not prevent you from calling the `eval()` family of methods locally, so it's a good safety measure to get in the habit of using.

Access Control Lists (ACLs)

With our servers now able to withstand some malicious attacks, the next step is to decide who can and cannot access the services we are providing. Enter access control lists (ACLs). An ACL specifies which clients are allowed access and which are denied. This is done with a simple `Array` defining these relationships. Let's add an ACL to our "Hello World" application. We know that we want only two machines to access the server—the server itself and the client. All other machines on the network should not be given access. Our server has the internal IP address of 192.168.1.12, and our client has the IP address of 192.168.1.7. Here is what our `HelloWorldServer` code now looks like:

```ruby
require 'drb'
require 'drb/acl'

# Make sure no one can call eval() and related methods remotely!
$SAFE = 1

class HelloWorldServer
```

```
def say_hello
  "Hello, world!"
end

end

acl = ACL.new(%w{deny all allow 192.168.1.12 allow 192.168.1.7})
DRb.install_acl(acl)

DRb.start_service("druby://192.168.1.12:61676", HelloWorldServer.new)
DRb.thread.join
```

So what have we changed with our `HelloWorldServer`? First, we can see that we are now requiring `'drb/acl'`. This gives us access to the `ACL` class we need to create so that we can tell `DRb` who is and is not allowed access. Second, we need to create a new `ACL`. `ACL.new` takes an `Array` that represents the deny/allow list:

```
acl = ACL.new(%w{deny all allow 192.168.1.12 allow 192.168.1.7})
```

Because we know our requirement is to ban all access, except to our two known IP addresses, we start with `deny all`. That blocks everybody. Next we need to open it to the two IP addresses we want to allow in by using `allow 192.168.1.12 allow 192.168.1.7`. As you can see, the `ACL` class expects the `Array` you give it to follow the pattern of *directive* (allow/deny) and then *address* or `all`.

After we have defined our `ACL`, we need to install it:

```
DRb.install_acl(acl)
```

It is probably worth pointing out at this point that when you install an `ACL` for `DRb`, `ACL` applies to the entire Ruby VM that is running that code. This is important if you want to have different ACLs for different services. In that case, you would need to run the different services using different Ruby VM instances so that you can install the appropriate ACL for each service.

We have also modified where the server binds itself to. We are no longer binding it to the IP address 127.0.0.1, but rather to 192.168.1.12. We do this so that our client can find it on 192.168.1.12; otherwise, we would get a "connection refused" error.

Now, if we were to run our client code for the "Hello World" application on a machine that had an IP address of, say, 192.168.1.6, we would get the following error:

```
DRb::DRbConnError: connection closed
```

Success! We have blocked that IP address from being able to use our service. It's important to note that the request actually made it all the way to the service on 192.168.1.12, into the DRb innards. It was refused only after the ACL was checked. This means that it is possible for a machine to run a denial-of-service attack on the service and potentially bring down the service.

Another thing that is worth mentioning about the ACL system in DRb is that the order in which you define the list is important. Let's reverse our example. Let's say we want to allow all machines on the network access to our service, except for the IP address 192.168.1.7. We could try to define our ACL like this:

```
acl = ACL.new(%w{allow all deny 192.168.1.7})
```

That should allow all machines through, except for 192.168.1.7. However, if you were to fire up the client on 192.168.1.7, you would be disappointed to see that the client works just fine. "Ah," you say to yourself. "I see what happened here. Because I put the allow all before deny 192.168.1.7, allow all is superseding deny and allowing all addresses through." So let's see what happens if we rewrite the ACL to look like this:

```
acl = ACL.new(%w{deny 192.168.1.7 allow all})
```

That should work, shouldn't it? It should block 192.168.1.7 and prevent the client from working. Well, if you run the client on that IP address, you'll see that it again runs with no problems. What is the reason for this? Well, when we give the ACL class the directive allow all, it does just that. It grants access to all machines and disregards what you have listed in the deny directive. Here's the correct way to write this ACL:

```
acl = ACL.new(%w{deny 192.168.1.7})
```

This denies only 192.168.1.7 and lets all other addresses through. The reverse of this action, just trying to allow addresses without any deny directives, does not work, however. The only way to prevent access is to use the deny directive. The allow directive alone does not imply deny all.

DRb over SSL

SSL (Secure Sockets Layer) has proven to be a great way to protect data as it travels across a network. Our distributed applications might be sending all sorts of sensitive information back and forth, so making sure that information is as secure and hacker-free as possible is definitely a good thing. This is where SSL comes in.

Although this book is not about encryption and network protocols, a simple explanation of how SSL works might prove helpful for the following section. In its simplest form SSL works like this: The client makes an SSL request to the server. The server says, "Here is my public key. Use it to encrypt your request, and I, the server, will use my private key to decode it." Because only the server has the private key, it is the only one that can decode the encrypted message the client just sent. That is a gross oversimplification of the process, but it should help make the following text a bit easier to understand. Of course, if you are still confused, or if you just want to find out more about how encryption and SSL work, plenty of great books and online tutorials are available.

Generating SSL Certificates

Chances are if you are reading this sidebar, you are unaccustomed to generating SSL certificates and can use a little help. Eric Hodel has created a simple Ruby utility for generating self-signed certificates called QuickCert. The certificates used in this book were generated using this utility. QuickCert can be found on Eric's website: http://segment7. net/projects/ruby/QuickCert/. After you install it, Quick-Cert looks for a file called qc_config in the directory in which you will run the QuickCert binary. The qc_config file used for this book looks like this:

```
full_hostname = `hostname`.strip
domainname = full_hostname.split('.')[1..-
1].join('.')
hostname = full_hostname.split('.')[0]

CA[:hostname] = hostname
CA[:domainname] = domainname
CA[:CA_dir] = File.join Dir.pwd, "CA"
```

```
CA[:password] = '1234'

CERTS << {
  :type => 'server',
  :hostname => 'hello-server',
  :password => '5678',
}

CERTS << {
  :type => 'client',
  :user => 'hello-client',
  :email => 'hello@example.com',
}
```

With this file in your current working directory, you would
simply run the QuickCert command:

```
$ QuickCert
```

This generates the following files:

```
CA/
    cacert.pem
    crl/
    newcerts/
            cert_1.pem
            cert_2.pem
    private/
            cakeypair.pem
    serial
hello-client/
            cert_hello-client.pem
            csr_hello-client.pem
            hello-client_keypair.pem
hello-server/
            cert_hello-server.pem
            csr_hello-server.pem
            hello-server_keypair.pem
```

Those are all the files you will need for the examples in this
part of the book.

Our "Hello World" application is a great candidate to be accessed over SSL. After all, we don't want just anyone seeing our super-secret message. Let's revisit our server to see what changes we have to make to allow it to accept SSL connections:

```
require 'drb'
require 'drb/ssl'

# Make sure no one can call eval() and related methods remotely!
$SAFE = 1

class HelloWorldServer

  def say_hello
    "Hello, world!"
  end

end

config = {
  :SSLPrivateKey =>
    OpenSSL::PKey::RSA.new(
      File.read("hello-server/hello-server_keypair.pem")
    ),
  :SSLCertificate =>
    OpenSSL::X509::Certificate.new(
      File.read("hello-server/cert_hello-server.pem")
    ),
}

DRb.start_service("drbssl://127.0.0.1:61676", HelloWorldServer.new,
config)
DRb.thread.join
```

The first noticeable change is that we need to require drb/ssl. That will give us access to the necessary libraries for DRb over SSL to work. Jumping down a bit, we are creating a Hash called config, which we will use to define our SSL parameters for the server. We need to define two parameters, :SSLPrivateKey and :SSLCertificate. As its name suggests, :SSLPrivateKey is the private key that the server needs to decode all the messages it receives. Using the OpenSSL libraries that come with the standard Ruby library, we create a new OpenSSL::PKey::RSA object and read in from disk our private key. The :SSLCertificate parameter is how we tell the server

what certificate to use. That certificate is sent to the client so that the client can
encrypt messages to send back to the server. Again, using the OpenSSL libraries, we
read in our certificate file and create a new OpenSSL::X509::Certificate object.

Previously when we started the service, we would use the following line of code:

```
DRb.start_service("druby://127.0.0.1:61676", HelloWorldServer.new)
```

Now we are using this:

```
DRb.start_service("drbssl://127.0.0.1:61676", HelloWorldServer.new,
  config)
```

This line contains two changes. We are now using the protocol drbssl instead of
druby when specifying the host to bind the service to. Also, we are passing in our
config Hash as the last parameter to the start_service method.

Now that our server is up and running, let's update our client to talk to the server
over SSL:

```
require 'drb'
require 'drb/ssl'

config = {
  :SSLVerifyMode => OpenSSL::SSL::VERIFY_PEER,
  :SSLCACertificateFile => "CA/cacert.pem",
}

DRb.start_service(nil, nil, config)
server = DRbObject.new_with_uri("drbssl://127.0.0.1:61676")

puts server.say_hello
```

Unlike our server code, our client code has changed significantly from our original version. As with our server, we need to require the drb/ssl libraries. Also, as with
our server, we need to create a Hash of parameters to help DRb understand how to connect to our server over SSL. We create a Hash called config and give it two parameters: :SSLVerifyMode and :SSLCACertificateFile. :SSLVerifyMode is set to
OpenSSL::SSL::VERIFY_PEER. This tells SSL to drop the connection if the peer
cannot be verified, usually because of a certificate mismatch or poorly signed certificate. We use :SSLCACertificateFile to point to the location of a certificate signed

by a Certificate Authority (CA).[1] In the world of the Internet and web browsers, the server usually sends this certificate during the initial SSL request, but because this isn't a web request, we already need access to this certificate locally.

Next we come to a line we are only used to seeing in the servers we have been writing:

```
DRb.start_service(nil, nil, config)
```

Why do we now need to add this line to our client? The answer is somewhat simple. We need to tell DRb how to configure our SSL, just like we did in the HelloWorld- Server class. The difference here is that we don't need to bind it to a specific host or port,[2] and we don't need to give it an instance of a "server" class we want to bind to that host and port. But we do want to pass it that Hash of parameters we created called config. After that we simply need to change our protocol from druby to drbssl when we call DRbObject.new_with_uri, similar to the change we made in our HelloWorldServer class.

Now our server and client are talking to each other over SSL. If you would like to test whether SSL is working, simply remove the :SSLCACertificateFile parame- ter from the configuration Hash on the client, and run it again. You will get an error not too dissimilar from the following:

```
DRb::DRbConnError: drbssl://127.0.0.1:61676 -
#<OpenSSL::SSL::SSLError: SSL_connect returned=1 errno=0
state=SSLv3 read server certificate B: certificate verify failed>
```

This proves that the client and server are attempting to speak with one another over SSL. It should also be pointed out that if we were to alter our original client applica- tion to look like this:

```
require 'drb'

server = DRbObject.new_with_uri("drbssl://127.0.0.1:61676")

puts server.say_hello
```

a friendly greeting of "Hello, world!" would be printed to the screen. This occurs because we have set up our server to accept connections over SSL, but we have not told it that it should accept only SSL connections, and those connections should be "authorized" connections. To make this happen, both sides need to verify the other side, so both the client and server need to present a CA certificate. Both sides also need to present both a key and a server certificate. This means that we have to alter both our server and client code.

Our server code should now look like the following:

```
require 'drb'
require 'drb/ssl'

# Make sure no one can call eval() and related methods remotely!
$SAFE = 1

class HelloWorldServer

  def say_hello
    "Hello, world!"
  end

end

config = {
  :SSLPrivateKey =>
    OpenSSL::PKey::RSA.new(
      File.read("hello-server/hello-server_keypair.pem")
    ),
  :SSLCertificate =>
    OpenSSL::X509::Certificate.new(
      File.read("hello-server/cert_hello-server.pem")
    ),
  :SSLVerifyMode => OpenSSL::SSL::VERIFY_PEER |
              OpenSSL::SSL::VERIFY_FAIL_IF_NO_PEER_CERT,
  :SSLCACertificateFile => "CA/cacert.pem"
}

DRb.start_service("drbssl://127.0.0.1:61676", HelloWorldServer.new,
config)
DRb.thread.join
```

Here we have added two more configuration parameters to our config Hash. The first is :SSLVerifyMode, which we have set to OpenSSL::SSL::VERIFY_PEER and OpenSSL::SSL::VERIFY_FAIL_IF_NO_PEER_CERT. This tells the server to drop the

connection to the client if that client cannot be verified or if that client does not present a certificate to the server. Like the original SSL client we wrote, we now need to
present a CA certificate, only this time it is on the server side. We do this with the
:SSLCACertificateFile parameter.

Our client also needs a bit of updating. If we were to run the client code in its
current state, we would get an error like the following:

```
DRb::DRbConnError: drbssl://127.0.0.1:61676 -
#<OpenSSL::SSL::SSLError: SSL_connect returned=1 errno=0
state=SSLv3 read finished A: sslv3 alert handshake failure>
```

We receive this error because the server now expects the client to present a key and
certificate to validate itself. Our client code should now be updated to look like the
following:

```
require 'drb'
require 'drb/ssl'

config = {
  :SSLVerifyMode => OpenSSL::SSL::VERIFY_PEER,
  :SSLCACertificateFile => "CA/cacert.pem",
  :SSLPrivateKey =>
    OpenSSL::PKey::RSA.new(
      File.read("hello-client/hello-client_keypair.pem")
    ),
  :SSLCertificate =>
    OpenSSL::X509::Certificate.new(
      File.read("hello-client/cert_hello-client.pem")
    )
}

DRb.start_service(nil, nil, config)
server = DRbObject.new_with_uri("drbssl://127.0.0.1:61676")

puts server.say_hello
```

In the configuration Hash for our client code, we have added the following two
parameters: :SSLPrivateKey and :SSLCertificate. As explained earlier, the
:SSLPrivateKey parameter tells DRb which private key to use when setting up SSL,
and the :SSLCertificate parameter tells DRb which certificate to use. Now, if we

were to run our client, we would get our familiar "Hello, world!" greeting. With that, we have now locked down our "Hello World" application to not only accept connections of SSL, but also to accept only trusted connections of SSL.

In Summary

In this section we first looked at how DRb's biggest advantage, its capability to easily invoke methods on a remote server, can also be a huge security concern. We demonstrated how easy it would be to have malicious code run that would delete the entire contents of the server. We solved that problem by setting Ruby's $SAFE level to a minimum of 1.

Next we looked at how access control lists (ACLs) can help secure your services further by limiting who can and cannot gain access to that service. We looked at the subtle nuances of how to build those ACLs and how they affect the entire Ruby VM running the service, not just the service you were hoping to install an ACL for.

We moved on to securing our DRb transactions by setting up communication between our client and server over SSL. We first set up our server to accept any connection of SSL, and then later we locked it down further to allow only authorized connections over SSL.

So although we have managed to lock down our services quite well, there is still opportunity for malicious behavior to creep in, just like with all applications. Careful planning, architecture, and testing will help, but there is no magic bullet to prevent security breaches.

ID Conversion

Earlier we talked about objects that get passed by reference. We said that when a message is called on a referenced object, the message is sent back to the server and is called against the original object. This is fundamentally true. What actually happens under the covers is that an ID for the referenced object, along with the message (say_hello), is sent back to the server. The server then uses that ID to find the original object in the ObjectSpace and to call the message on it.

The method of looking up an object in the ObjectSpace using the reference ID is called ID conversion. DRb ships with three built-in ID converters: DRb::DRbId-Conv, DRb::TimerIdConv, and DRb::GWIdConv. It is also possible to build your own ID converter, as you will see a little later. Depending on which ID converter you build, it can change how objects are looked up in the ObjectSpace, as well as how, and when, those objects get garbage-collected.

Built-in ID Converters

Although DRb ships with three built-in ID converters, we will only look at DRb::DRbIdConv and DRb::TimerIdConv. The general consensus on the DRb::GWIdConv converter is that it is extremely complicated to set up, prone to failure, and quite slow. For that reason, I won't cover it. Instead, we'll look at building our own custom ID converter a little later.

DRb::DRbIdConv

DRb::DRbIdConv is the default ID converter when dealing with DRb. We saw an example of this earlier when we were writing our "User Server" application. When we inspected our User object, we saw the following:

```
#<DRb::DRbObject:0x81ed4 @uri="druby://127.0.0.1:61676", @ref=265930>
```

If we look at the @ref instance variable, we see that it is set to 265930—the ID of the referenced object living on the server. The default ID converter, DRb::DRbId-Conv, simply uses the object_id for the object to determine its reference. That reference ID is then used to look up the object in the ObjectSpace and then invoke the requested message.

Let's rewrite our HelloWorldServer to see this in practice:

```
require 'drb'

class HelloWorldServer

  def say_hello
    hello = Hello.new
    puts "hello.object_id: #{hello.object_id}"
    hello
  end
```

```
  end

  class Hello
    include DRbUndumped

    def to_s
      "Hello, world!"
    end

  end

  DRb.start_service("druby://127.0.0.1:61676", HelloWorldServer.new)
  DRb.thread.join
```

The big change we have made is in the say_hello method. Instead of returning a simple String, we are now returning a Hello object. We have told Hello to include DRbUndumped so that we get a reference to the object on the server when we retrieve it from the client. Finally, so that we can validate that the object_id is indeed being used as the reference ID, we print it to the screen with this:

```
  puts "hello.object_id: #{hello.object_id}"
```

Let's update our client so that we can use the new Hello object we are now receiving:

```
  require 'drb'

  server = DRbObject.new_with_uri("druby://127.0.0.1:61676")

  hello = server.say_hello

  puts hello.inspect
```

If we were to run this, we would see something like the following printed from the client:

```
  #<DRb::DRbObject:0x822e4 @uri="druby://127.0.0.1:61676", @ref=265410>
```

On the server side, we see something similar to the following:

```
  "hello.object_id: 265410"
```

As we can see, the `object_id` on the server printout matches the `@ref` instance variable on the `DRbObject` we received from the server. This is the default because it is incredibly easy to make sense of how the reference ID is created and how it is mapped on the server side. It is also pretty efficient to grab the object from the `ObjectSpace` using the `object_id`, so there is definitely a performance win to be had using this default ID converter.

DRb::TimerIdConv

The default ID converter, `DRb::DRbIdConv`, has one downside. If you're not careful, referenced objects on the server can become garbage-collected and are no longer available when the client tries to reference them. Although the client has a pointer to the local `DRb::DRbObject` it got from the server, the server itself may no longer have a pointer to the object that is referenced from the client. In that case it becomes eligible for garbage collection. One solution to this problem is to use the `DRb::TimerIdConv` class.

The only difference between `DRb::TimerIdConv` and `DRb::DRbIdConv` is that `DRb::TimerIdConv` tells the server to keep its objects alive for a certain amount of time after they were last accessed. The default length for this keepalive is 600 seconds, or 10 minutes.

Because of the nature of this ID converter, it's rather difficult to show a good working example of objects being garbage-collected by the server and the server losing the reference to them, and so on. What we can look at is how to install a new ID converter for our HelloWorldServer:

```
require 'drb'
require 'drb/timeridconv'

class HelloWorldServer

  def say_hello
    Hello.new
  end

end

class Hello
  include DRbUndumped
```

```
  def to_s
    "Hello, world!"
  end

end

DRb.install_id_conv(DRb::TimerIdConv.new(30))
DRb.start_service("druby://127.0.0.1:61676", HelloWorldServer.new)
DRb.thread.join
```

Our updated server code has two important lines. The first is where we require
`DRb::TimerIdConv` with `require 'drb/timeridconv'`. The second is the following line:

```
DRb.install_id_conv(DRb::TimerIdConv.new(30))
```

With this line we tell DRb to use an instance of `DRb::TimerIdConv` that has a timeout of 30 seconds. Because we used the `install_id_conv` method, we have told the
Ruby VM that is running our server that any DRb services in that VM should use the
`DRb::TimerIdConv` converter. Later, when we talk about creating a custom ID converter, we'll learn how to assign a particular ID converter to a particular service,
despite what is configured as the global converter for that VM.

At this point you might wonder why you shouldn't use the `DRb::TimerIdConv`
class all the time. If it helps protect you from garbage collection, isn't that something
you want? The answer is yes and no. It's always a good idea to make sure your objects
are there when you reference them. However, think about what happens when you use
this particular ID converter. You tell the Ruby VM to not garbage-collect those objects
for a minimum of N seconds after the last time that object was touched. If you have
a high-traffic service, you could quickly increase your memory usage while Ruby holds
on to all these objects that you may or may not need to have hanging around.

A better approach to solve the garbage-collection problem lies in your architecture. Don't take an object from the server and hold onto it in the client for any longer
than you absolutely need to. Retrieve the object from the server, use it, and then get
rid of it. If you want to make sure you have access to that same referenced object minutes, hours, or days later, you should consider writing your own custom ID converter
that stores your objects in something other than the `ObjectSpace`.

Building Your Own ID Converter

Now that we have looked at a couple of different ID converters, we can create our own custom ID converter. Why would we want to do that? Perhaps we want to have some sort of signature in the ID so that we can tell by looking at it where it originated. Perhaps we are using a database as our object store on the server, and we want to use the primary key for the database row as the ID. Or perhaps we just want to be different. Whatever the motivation, it is easy to create a custom ID converter.

In our custom ID converter, we just want to append HW: to the object_id for our objects so that we know that those objects came from the HelloWorldServer. Here is what our ID converter would look like:

```
class CustomIdConv

  def to_id(obj)
    "HW:#{obj.object_id}"
  end

  def to_obj(ref)
    ObjectSpace._id2ref(ref.gsub(/^HW:/, '').to_i)
  end

end
```

For an ID converter to work in DRb, it needs to respond to two methods—to_obj and to_id. Looking at to_id first, we can see that it takes an object. Our to_id method returns a new String that simply concatenates HW: to the object_id, which returns something like HW:12345. Our to_obj is a little more complex, but it is still relatively straightforward. The method takes a reference ID, HW:12345, and strips HW:, leaving us with 12345. We have to convert the 12345 String to an Integer so that we can pass it to the _id2ref method on Object-Space. The _id2ref method on ObjectSpace retrieves the referenced object from the proper memory location in the Ruby VM and returns it.

As you saw earlier, when we talked about DRb::TimerIdConv, installing a new ID converter is simple. We can install our custom ID converter like so:

```
DRb.install_id_conv(CustomIdConv.new)
```

Now, if we were to run our client, we would see something like the following print to the screen:

```
#<DRb::DRbObject:0x822bc @uri="druby://127.0.0.1:61676",
 @ref="HW:264770">
```

Using Multiple ID Converters

Earlier I mentioned that when you install a converter using the `DRb.install_id_conv` method, you tell DRb that all services in that Ruby VM are now to use that particular ID converter. What happens if you want to use multiple ID converters? The solution is quite simple.

If you remember when we talked about setting up a service to work over SSL, you learned that the `start_service` method takes a third parameter, a `Hash` of configuration parameters. One parameter in the list of available parameters is `:idconv`, which tells DRb to use a particular ID converter for that service and that service alone:

```
DRb.start_service("druby://127.0.0.1:61676", HelloWorldServer.new,
 {:idconv => CustomIdConv.new})
DRb.start_service("druby://127.0.0.1:61677", HelloWorldServer.new)
```

Here we have set up two instances of our `HelloWorldServer`. The first instance, on port 61676, will use our `CustomIdConv` class. The second instance, on port 61677, will use the default ID converter, `DRb::DRbIdConv`.

Let's write a client so that we can see the different ID converters in practice:

```
require 'drb'

s1 = DRbObject.new_with_uri("druby://127.0.0.1:61676")
s2 = DRbObject.new_with_uri("druby://127.0.0.1:61677")

puts s1.say_hello.inspect
puts s2.say_hello.inspect
```

When we run our client, we should see something like the following printed:

```
#<DRb::DRbObject:0x820dc @uri="druby://127.0.0.1:61676",
 @ref="HW:264380">
#<DRb::DRbObject:0x818d0 @uri="druby://127.0.0.1:61677", @ref=262660>
```

As you can see, our first `Hello` object has a reference of `"HW:264380"`, the format used by our `CustomIdConv` class. The second `Hello` object has a simpler reference of `262660`. Because the reference on the second `Hello` object is not prepended with `HW:`, we know that it is not using our `CustomIdConv` class, but rather the default `DRb::DRbIdConv` ID converter.

In Summary

In this section we talked about a couple of built-in ID converters—the default ID converter, `DRb::DRbIdConv`, and the timer-based converter, `DRb::TimerIdConv`. We discussed the possibility of referenced objects no longer being available because they have been garbage-collected, and a couple of potential solutions. You learned how to install a new ID converter for all the services in a particular Ruby VM, as well as how to use a custom converter for a particular service. Finally, you created your own custom ID converter.

Conclusion

This chapter has given you your first taste of distributed programming with Ruby using the DRb library that is bundled with the standard install of Ruby. We started with a simple "Hello World" application and built on that to add security, proprietary Ruby objects, and custom ID conversion.

You also learned valuable lessons about some of the pitfalls of the DRb library so that you can avoid them in your code. For example, you learned how easy it is to execute malicious code on a DRb service. You also learned how to prevent that situation.

With what you have learned in this first chapter, you can build successful, small-scale, distributed applications. The next chapter, on `Rinda`, builds on what you have learned about DRb. You will learn how to add features such as automatic lookup of your services, callbacks and notifications, and more.

Endnotes

1. A trusted Certificate Authority (CA) ensures that the certificate holder is actually who he claims to be. Without a trusted signed certificate, your data may be encrypted, but the party you are communicating with may not be who you think. Without certificates, impersonation attacks would be much more common.

2. Although we don't need to bind the service to a host/port, DRb automatically binds it to a random port locally. Whether this is a feature or poor implementation, I'll leave up to you. Just be aware that a service started on `127.0.0.1:random_port` now is serving up a `nil` object.

CHAPTER 2

Rinda

Chapter 1, "Distributed Ruby (DRb)," explored the DRb package that ships with Ruby. You used DRb to quickly build distributed applications. Although those applications were certainly functional and easy to code, they lacked a few key features and presented a few problems.

When reviewing all of our DRb applications, you will notice, for a start, that we hardcoded IP addresses and ports into both our servers and clients. This type of tight coupling of applications can be problematic in both production and development. It can make fault tolerance difficult to code for. And what do you do if you need to start the service on a different machine that has a different IP address? We could also create and attempt to maintain complex configurations, but in the modern world of cloud computing IP addresses fluctuate every time you launch an instance. So, keeping those configuration files up to date would be extremely complicated and prone to error. That is certainly not an option.

What about finding out what services, as a client, are available in our world of distributed applications? Again, we have been hardcoding our connection to the service we want to use. Let's use a simple example. Say we want to send an email to a customer. We do that by writing to a mail service we have somewhere. What happens if that mail service is down and we want to write to a backup mail service? Do we just wait for the first call to time out, catch the exception, and then write to the backup? What if the backup is also down? Another timeout? Another exception? We need a way to get a listing of services that is available to us and then choose the correct service to use, or quickly raise an error.

Enter Rinda, a Ruby port of the Linda[1] distributed computing paradigm. This paradigm allows an application, through the use of a RingServer, to detect and interact with other services on the network. This should help us solve some of the problems we were facing with our earlier DRb applications.

"Hello World" the Rinda Way

Let's start by reviewing the "Hello World" application we built in Chapter 1. This will be a great way to see how a simple DRb application and a simple Rinda application differ.

I mentioned earlier that Rinda makes use of a RingServer. A RingServer is essentially a central clearinghouse for services, as shown in Figure 2-1. The life cycle for a typical RingServer with one service and one client basically goes something like this: The client asks the RingServer where to find a particular service. The RingServer responds with the service's address. The client and service then communicate directly with each other (see Figure 2-2). The specifics are as follows:

1. The RingServer starts and begins listening on a broadcast UDP[2] address.

2. A service creates a RingFinger that looks up and finds a broadcasting RingServer.

3. The service tells the RingServer where to find itself (for example, 127.0.0.1:8000), as well as what services it offers.

4. A client wants to find the service, so it also creates a RingFinger that again looks up and finds the RingServer.

5. The client tells the RingServer what kind of service it is looking for by using a Tuple template.

6. The RingServer responds by giving the client direct access to the original service on 127.0.0.1:8000.

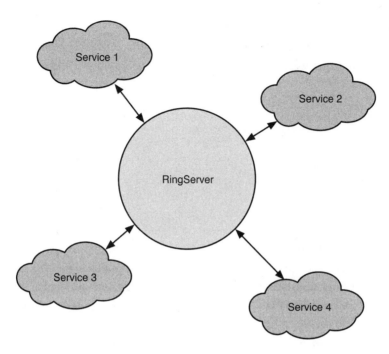

Figure 2-1   Services list themselves with a central RingServer, which then coordinates all communication between the services.

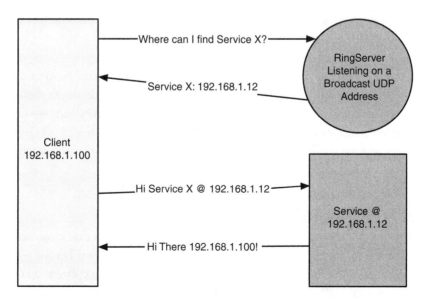

Figure 2-2   The typical request life cycle of Rinda applications.

Building a `RingServer` is straightforward and simple. In Chapter 3, "RingyDingy," we'll discuss RingyDingy, a library that makes it even easier to use RingServers; but first we should write our own so we can understand exactly what it does.

```
require 'rinda/ring'
require 'rinda/tuplespace'

DRb.start_service
Rinda::RingServer.new(Rinda::TupleSpace.new)
DRb.thread.join
```

Looking at the code for our `RingServer`, it should quickly leap out at you that we are making DRb calls. Why is that, you might ask? Simple. `Rinda` sits on top of the DRb library. This is great news for us, because we already understand how to use DRb. When we see lines like `DRb.start_service` and `DRb.thread.join`, we already know what they do. That allows us to focus on the actual `RingServer` portion of this code.

First we need to require the `Rinda` libraries. In particular, we need to require `rinda/ring` and `rinda/tuplespace`. Once we've done that and started the DRb service, we can start our `RingServer` with the following line:

```
Rinda::RingServer.new(Rinda::TupleSpace.new)
```

When we create our `RingServer`, we pass it a new `Rinda::TupleSpace` class. A TupleSpace[3] essentially manages access to the `Tuples`[4] it contains. Before I explain what a `TupleSpace` and a `Tuple` are, I would like to point out that even though we are starting a server, we did not have to bind the `RingServer` to any IP address or port. By default the `RingServer` binds to port 7647. You can change that by passing in an optional second parameter to the new method on `Rinda::RingServer`, like this:

```
Rinda::RingServer.new(Rinda::TupleSpace.new, 8080)
```

Now the `RingServer` will bind itself to port 8080.

Now, let's talk about `TupleSpaces` and `Tuples`. I said earlier that a `TupleSpace` manages access to the `Tuples` it contains. But what does that mean? Let me give you an analogy that might make this a bit clearer. When you go into a coffee shop or grocery store, inevitably a bulletin board near the front door has a bunch of flyers pinned to it, advertising everything from guitar lessons to roommates to underwater basket-weaving courses. People come along and search the bulletin board, looking for something they need, or perhaps for a bit of a giggle. If they find a posting they like, they can either take it off the board so that no one else will see it, or they can make a copy for themselves and leave the original up there for others to see. We can think of a `TupleSpace` as that bulletin board. It is a place where we can post our services. The flyer is like the `Tuple`. In our current example we would be posting a "Hello World" service `Tuple` to the `TupleSpace`.

So, armed with a basic understanding of the world of `TupleSpaces` and `Tuples`, we can start to rewrite our "Hello World" service using `Rinda`. It should be noted that for the examples in this chapter to work, you must have a `RingServer` running in the background. It is also important to remember to restart your `RingServer` between each new example to avoid potentially confusing results. We will be iterating on many of these examples—if we don't start/stop all our services between each build, things might start to get a bit confusing.

For now, let's rebuild that "Hello World" service that we originally built in Chapter 1. Here is what our "Hello World" service originally looked like:

```
require 'drb'

class HelloWorldServer

  def say_hello
    "Hello, world!"
  end

end

DRb.start_service("druby://127.0.0.1:61676",
                  HelloWorldServer.new)
DRb.thread.join
```

Now let's look at what this service will look like when we rewrite it using `Rinda`:

```
require 'rinda/ring'

class HelloWorldServer
  include DRbUndumped
```

```
  def say_hello
    "Hello, world!"
  end

end

DRb.start_service
ring_server = Rinda::RingFinger.primary
ring_server.write([:hello_world_service, :HelloWorldServer,
                   HelloWorldServer.new,
                   'I like to say hi!'],
                 Rinda::SimpleRenewer.new)

DRb.thread.join
```

Again you can see that we need to require the rinda/ring class. Our HelloWorldServer class shouldn't look that different from what we are used to, except that we are now including the DRbUndumped module. Because we will send an instance of the HelloWorldServer class across the wire to the RingServer, we need to pass it by reference and not by value so that we don't cause any exceptions on the client end if it doesn't have the HelloWorldServer class definition. And chances are pretty good that the client won't have the class definition for it, so why set ourselves up for errors?

After we start the DRb service, we find the RingServer we started earlier. We do that by calling the primary method on the Rinda::RingFinger class, which will retrieve the first RingServer it finds. Rinda::RingFinger is used by clients and other services to find the TupleSpace for a RingServer. Later in this chapter we will look at how to select a specific RingServer, but for now we have only one RingServer, so the primary method will work just fine.

After we have a RingServer, we can write our Tuple into it. The next section discusses creating Tuple templates at greater length, so we won't go into much detail right now, except to say that we have given our service a set of parameters to describe our server and an instance of the HelloWorldServer to serve up.

Although it is definitely a bit more complicated than our original DRb version of the HelloWorldServer, this implementation will eventually lead to greater flexibility down the line. For example, have you noticed that we have not bound ourselves to a specific IP address or port? That's because we passed our Tuple Array template into the write method on the RingServer. We have told the RingServer, "Here is my service, and you can find me here."

So how does all of this affect our client?

```
require 'rinda/ring'

DRb.start_service
ring_server = Rinda::RingFinger.primary

service = ring_server.read([:hello_world_service, nil, nil, nil])
server = service[2]

puts server.say_hello

puts service.inspect
```

Because we know what the first few lines of this code do, let's jump to the following line:

```
service = ring_server.read([:hello_world_service, nil, nil, nil])
```

In our server code we called the `write` method on the `RingServer`, passing it a `Tuple` template. Now we are calling the `read` method and passing it a variation of our `Tuple` template. In the next section we'll discuss `Tuples` and `TupleSpaces` in more depth. For now, please accept the explanation that a `nil` used in a `Tuple` template is the equivalent of a wildcard search, so we are basically asking for the first `Tuple` that matches `:hello_world_service` as the first parameter.

Now that you have a basic understanding of how to use `Tuple` templates, we can get back to our "Hello World" application. After we have retrieved a `Tuple` from the `RingServer`, we need to get the `HelloWorldServer` instance out of the `Tuple` `Array` with `server = service[2]`. It might seem odd that in order to retrieve our `HelloWorldServer` instance from the `Tuple` we retrieved from the `RingServer` using an `Array` syntax, `service[2]`, it does, in fact, make sense. We stored an `Array` containing the original description of the service and the instance of the `HelloWorldServer` in the `RingServer` as an `Array`, the index of the `HelloWorld-Server` is 2. When we run our client, it should produce output like this:

```
Hello, world!
[:hello_world_service, :HelloWorldServer, #<DRb::DRbObject:0x75c24
  @ref=243680, @uri="druby://192.168.1.12:55620">, "I like to say hi!"]
```

If we examine the inspect on the service, we can see that the Tuple Array that is returned from the RingServer matches the one we placed into. We can also see that the HelloWorldServer instance is being passed by reference and not by value because of our use of the DRbUndumped module. You can also see that the "Hello World" server is running on 192.168.1.12:55620. That was the IP address of the machine running the server, and the port was picked basically at random.

In Summary

In this section you started to get your feet wet with Rinda. You gained a basic understanding of RingServers, and you were introduced to the ideas of TupleSpaces and Tuples. We also managed to decouple our code so that we didn't have to hardcode IP addresses and ports, and instead we were able to dynamically find the service we wanted.

Understanding Tuples and TupleSpaces

In the preceding section we talked briefly about TupleSpaces. We used the analogy of a bulletin board to demonstrate how a TupleSpace works. Like a bulletin board, TupleSpaces allow us to perform a variety of tasks. We can write to a TupleSpace to post our service. Someone can come along and get a read-only copy of a service from that TupleSpace. We briefly looked at both of those examples when we re-created our "Hello World" application. But that is not all we can do with Tuple-Spaces. We can take a Tuple from the TupleSpace so that no one can see it. We can read all the Tuples, should we desire, just like with a bulletin board.

Writing a Tuple to a TupleSpace

Before we can look at reading and taking tuples from our TupleSpace, we need to create and write a Tuple to the TupleSpace. Creating a Tuple is quite easy. All you need to do is pass in an Array containing the template you want to store. Although this template can be of any size, and its values can be in any order, it is important to note that later, when you are trying to look up a service, you must match the template. This means that if you use an Array with ten entries as your Tuple template, you need to look it up later using an Array with ten entries, and those entries must all be in the same order. This will become clearer shortly as we look at our client code. With that said, there does seem to be a loose "standard" in the community of using a four-entry `Tuple` template with the following pattern: `[:name, :Class, instance_of_class, 'description']`. In our "Hello World" application, that translates into `Tuple: [:hello_world_service, :HelloWorldServer, HelloWorldServer.new, 'I like to say hi!']`. We would write that template like so:

```
ring_server.write([:hello_world_service, :HelloWorldServer,
                   HelloWorldServer.new,
                   'I like to say hi!'],
                   Rinda::SimpleRenewer.new)
```

Under the covers, `Rinda` takes the `Array` and creates the appropriate `Rinda::Tuple` class, so we don't have to worry about learning yet another class API. The `write` method also takes an optional second argument, which can be either an `Integer`, representing the number of seconds you want this `Tuple` to live, or a `Renewer`. We will discuss `Renewers` later in this chapter. Simply put, the second parameter to the `write` method determines how and when the `Tuple` gets expired.

> **Fun Fact**
>
> When passing in a `Tuple` to the `write` method of a `TupleSpace`, if you either pass in `nil` for the second argument or pass in no second argument, the `Tuple` will be set to expire at `Time.at(2**31-1)`. In human terms, the expiration date will be `Mon Jan 18 22:14:07 -0500 2038`. This date represents the date and time when UNIX clocks will stop functioning.[5]

Reading a Tuple from a TupleSpace

In our "Hello World" application server code, we called the `write` method on the `RingServer`, passing it a `Tuple` template. To retrieve that `Tuple` we call the `read` method and pass it a variation of our `Tuple` template. Because our original `Tuple` template had four entries, our client also has to pass in a `Tuple` template with four entries. When you pass in `nil` as an entry in a `Tuple` template, you're doing a wild-card search on any entry in that position. In our case we are asking for the first service whose first `Tuple` entry is `:hello_world_service`. We don't care what the other template entries are. Let me give a few examples to clarify this point. Let's look at this bit of code:

```ruby
require 'logger'
require 'rinda/ring'

DRb.start_service
ring_server = Rinda::RingFinger.primary

tuple1 = [:logging_service, :Logger,
          ::Logger.new(STDOUT), 'Primary Logger']
tuple2 = [:logging_service, :Logger,
          ::Logger.new(STDOUT), 'Secondary Logger']
tuple3 = [:syslog_service, :SysLogger,
          ::Logger.new(STDOUT), 'Primary Logger']

ring_server.write(tuple1, Rinda::SimpleRenewer.new)
ring_server.write(tuple2, Rinda::SimpleRenewer.new)
ring_server.write(tuple3, Rinda::SimpleRenewer.new)

logger = ring_server.read([nil, :Logger, nil, nil])

puts logger.inspect

logger = ring_server.read([nil, nil, nil, nil])

puts logger.inspect

logger = ring_server.read([nil, nil, nil, 'Primary Logger'])

puts logger.inspect

# DRb.thread.join
```

If we were to run this code, we would get something like the following:

```
[:logging_service, :Logger, #<DRb::DRbObject:0x54204 @ref=206640,
@uri="druby://192.168.1.12:55462">, "Primary Logger"]
[:logging_service, :Logger, #<DRb::DRbObject:0x53c8c @ref=206640,
@uri="druby://192.168.1.12:55462">, "Primary Logger"]
```

```
[:logging_service, :Logger, #<DRb::DRbObject:0x53714 @ref=206640,
@uri="druby://192.168.1.12:55462">, "Primary Logger"]
```

As you can see, we make three different requests for services, each with different `Tuple` templates. Yet each time we get back a reference to the first `Tuple` entry we created. When `Rinda` attempts to find a `Tuple` based on a `Tuple` template, it returns the first `Tuple` that matches the `Tuple` template passed into it. This should demonstrate the importance not only of using a consistent `Tuple` template, but also of writing your `Tuple` to be as specific as possible.

Variation: Using Hashes for Tuples

The "standard" way to create `Tuples` is to use the `Array` syntax we have been discussing, but it is also possible to use a `Hash` to represent the `Tuple`. The rules for using the `Hash` syntax are pretty much the same as for the `Array` syntax. If you provide a `Tuple` template with four keys, you must search using a `Hash` with the same four keys. You still use `nil` as the wildcard for each of the keys in the `Hash`, as you would do with the `Array` syntax. The only other restriction is that you have to use a `String` for the key and no other type of `Object`, including `Symbols`.

Let's see what our "Hello World" `Tuple` looks like using the `Hash` syntax:

```
ring_server.write({'service_name' =>
                   :hello_world_service,
                   'service_class' =>
                   :HelloWorldServer,
                   'service_instance' =>
                   HelloWorldServer.new,
                   'service_description' =>
                   'I like to say hi!'},
                 Rinda::SimpleRenewer.new
                 )
```

The reading of that `Tuple` would look something like this:

```
ring_server.read({'service_name' =>
                    :hello_world_service,
                'service_class' =>
                nil,
                'service_instance' =>
                nil,
                'service_description' =>
                    nil})
```

After you have a Tuple, you can retrieve the instance by doing something like this:

```
service['service_instance']
```

In my opinion, that is a lot easier to read than this:

```
service[2]
```

During the writing of this book, I came to enjoy the `Hash` syntax more than the `Array` syntax. I find that although it involves a bit more typing, it makes the code more readable. The only real downside, I've found, is that there is no "standard" naming convention for the keys to the `Hash`. So if you decide to use the `Hash` syntax, you also have to publish an API for the keys that the `Hash` expects. This is also somewhat true for the `Array` syntax. You can publish a `Tuple` of any size and with the elements in whatever order you want them. But as mentioned earlier, there does seem to be some consensus in the community about how an `Array`-based `Tuple` should be organized.

Taking a Tuple from a TupleSpace

Now that you have a firm grasp on how to `read` and `write` from our `TupleSpace`, let's see what happens when we throw a bit of concurrency into the mix. Let's look at a fairly contrived example. Let's build a "Counter Service." We will build a `Rinda` service that simply hosts an `Integer`, which will start at 0. Our client is responsible for incrementing that number by 1. First, the server:

```
require 'rinda/ring'

DRb.start_service
ring_server = Rinda::RingFinger.primary
ring_server.write([:count_service, 0],
                  Rinda::SimpleRenewer.new)

DRb.thread.join
```

Only two things are worth mentioning about our service. First, I used a nonstandard `Array` syntax for the `Tuple`. I only did that for the sake of brevity. The other thing worth mentioning, and this really goes for this whole example, is that the best way to solve our problem would be to let the server update the `Integer`. But that wouldn't be any fun. Instead, we will let our client do that:

```
require 'rinda/ring'

DRb.start_service
ring_server = Rinda::RingFinger.primary

threads = []

10.times do |th|
  threads << Thread.new do
    10.times do |i|
      service = ring_server.read([:count_service, nil])
      sleep(rand(5))
      puts "#{th}: #{i} (#{service.inspect})\n"
      updated_count = service[1] + 1
      puts "#{th}: #{i} (#{updated_count})\n"
      ring_server.write([:count_service, updated_count])
    end
  end
end

threads.each {|t| t.join}

service = ring_server.read([:count_service, nil])

puts service.inspect
```

In our client we will create ten different Threads. Each of those Threads reads the current Integer from the server. The client then sleeps for a random time between 0 and 5 seconds. When the client wakes up, it increments the Integer by 1 and writes that back to the server. Because we have ten Threads running, and each Thread loops through our code ten times, we should see the final count be 100. Let's see what happens when we run this code:

```
3: 0 ([:count_service, 0])
3: 0 (1)
6: 0 ([:count_service, 0])
5: 0 ([:count_service, 0])
6: 0 (1)
5: 0 (1)
...
2: 9 ([:count_service, 9])
2: 9 (10)
1: 8 ([:count_service, 10])
1: 8 (11)
1: 9 ([:count_service, 11])
1: 9 (12)
[:count_service, 12]
```

Well, I'm pretty sure that 12 does not equal 100! So what happened? Well, each time a Thread reads the Integer it got from the service, it holds onto that Integer, sleeps for a bit, and then updates that Integer and writes it back to the service. When it does that, it overwrites the previous Integer that another Thread placed in there while the first thread was sleeping. So now that we know what's happening, how can we fix it? Enter the take method. Let's rewrite our client to use the take method:

```
require 'rinda/ring'

DRb.start_service
ring_server = Rinda::RingFinger.primary

threads = []

10.times do |th|
  threads << Thread.new do
    10.times do |i|
```

```
      service = ring_server.take([:count_service, nil])
      sleep(rand(5))
      puts "#{th}: #{i} (#{service.inspect})\n"
      updated_count = service[1] + 1
      puts "#{th}: #{i} (#{updated_count})\n"
      ring_server.write([:count_service, updated_count])
    end
  end
end

threads.each {|t| t.join}

service = ring_server.read([:count_service, nil])

puts service.inspect
```

The only difference in our new client is the use of the take method instead of the read method. If we were to run this code, we would get something like the following:

```
1: 0 ([:count_service, 0])
1: 0 (1)
0: 0 ([:count_service, 1])
0: 0 (2)
2: 0 ([:count_service, 2])
2: 0 (3)
...
7: 9 ([:count_service, 97])
7: 9 (98)
8: 9 ([:count_service, 98])
8: 9 (99)
9: 9 ([:count_service, 99])
9: 9 (100)
[:count_service, 100]
```

That's more like it! 100 definitely equals 100. Very good. So what just happened? When you use the take method, you remove that Tuple from the server. When you do that, no one else can access it. Think back to our bulletin board example. If you take the flyer for guitar lessons off the board, no one else can see it. That is exactly what the take method does. Because each Thread takes the Tuple from the server, holds it while it sleeps, and then updates it and puts it back, it prevents the other threads from doing the same thing.

The question you should be asking is, if two `Threads` hit the service, and the first one calls the `take` method, gets the `Tuple`, and then sleeps, why doesn't the other raise an exception? Shouldn't the second `Thread` get back `nil` from the server, causing the rest of the code to blow up? The answer is, it does not get back `nil` from the server. In fact, what actually happens is that the second `Thread` just sits there and waits for the `take` method to return the `Tuple`. The `take` method is basically wrapped in a big infinite loop that keeps checking to see if the `Tuple` has been returned. When it is returned, the loop is broken, and the `Tuple` is returned to the client. In the real world, this code would hang forever while it waited for the `Tuple` if we never wrote it back. So it is wise to always wrap any `take` method calls in a `Timeout` to prevent your code from simply hanging.

Reading All Tuples in a TupleSpace

Earlier, when we spoke about the `read` method and how `Tuple` templates work, I said that the `read` method returns the first `Tuple` that matches the template. That's great, but what if you want to get back a list of services? The solution in `Rinda` is to use the `read_all` method. The `read_all` method behaves just like the `read` method, except that it returns an `Array` of `Arrays` representing all the services that match the template, instead of just a single `Array` representing the first matching template.

Let's look at a couple of examples. First, let's build a client that lists all the services that are available to us. I'll use the server code we wrote in the section about the `read` method that creates three different `Loggers`. Let's build a client that lists those for us:

```
require 'rinda/ring'

DRb.start_service
ring_server = Rinda::RingFinger.primary

services = ring_server.read_all([nil, nil, nil, nil])

puts "Services on #{ring_server.__drburi}"
services.each do |service|
  puts "#{service[0]}: #{service[1]} on #{service[2].__drburi} -
  #{service[3]}"
end
```

By passing the `read_all` method a `Tuple` template full of `nil`s, we are telling it to match all `Tuple` templates on the `RingServer`. We then print the `uri` of the `RingServer`. After we get the `Array` of services from the `RingServer`, we loop through each one and print a nicely formatted message telling us the name of the service, the type of class hosted there, where it's hosted, and a description of the service. The output from that code would look something like the following:

```
Services on druby://macbates.home:56017
logging_service: Logger on druby://192.168.1.12:56018 - Primary Logger
logging_service: Logger on druby://192.168.1.12:56018 - Secondary
  Logger
syslog_service: SysLogger on druby://192.168.1.12:56018 - Primary
  Logger
```

Listing the services available is just a simple example of how to use the `read_all` method. In our simple example we could use the `read_all` method to get a list of just the `Logger` instances available to us. Then, if a problem occurs with the first, primary `Logger`, we could just iterate through that list until we either found a working `Logger` or ran out of logging services that we could use.

In Summary

In this section you gained a deep understanding of how `TupleSpaces` and `Tuples` work in `Rinda`. We dove into the four main methods of interacting with `Tuples`: `write`, `read`, `take`, and `read_all`. We developed a `Thread`-safe application using the `take` method. Finally, we retrieved a list of services available to us and iterated through each one.

Callbacks and Observers

Callbacks and observers are evident in almost all languages, and most frameworks within those languages. They are a universal design pattern that allows a system to wait for another system or process to tell it that some event has occurred. The system that has been listening for that event can then choose to respond in some fashion. It could be that the system simply logs a message. Maybe it fires off an email or does some further process. Either way, it can be an incredibly useful design pattern to have access to.

In Ruby it is quite common for libraries to provide some sort of callback mechanism. One of the most significant examples of this is Ruby on Rails and its libraries. Ruby on Rails has introduced the concepts of notifications and callbacks to developers who would have otherwise been unaware of them and their power. The Ruby on Rails framework heavily relies on this design pattern to offer developers convenient hooks into the system so that they don't have to hack the code to enhance the system.

Understanding Callbacks

Let's look quickly at a simple `ActiveRecord` model. `ActiveRecord` is an Object Relational Mapping framework that ships with Ruby On Rails. Using `ActiveRecord` you can have a database model that looks as simple as this:

```
class User < ActiveRecord::Base
end
```

Assuming that the `users` table in the database has a `username` and a `password` column, you can create a new row in the `users` table as simply as this:

```
user = User.create(:username => 'markbates', :password => '123456')
user.save
```

Wow! Remarkable, but shouldn't we first encrypt the password before we save it to the database? What if you wanted to send a welcome email after the user was created? You could very easily encrypt the password before you send it to the `create` method on the user. You could also send the welcome email after you have called the `save` method. Those are definitely valid options. However, if you end up creating users in different parts of your application, you end up having that code repeated all over the place, and that is not very DRY.

Callbacks allow us to inject code at different parts of the event cycle to do the things we want. In our `ActiveRecord` example we could use the built-in callbacks system in `ActiveRecord` to allow us to encrypt the user's password and send him or her a welcome email:

```
class User < ActiveRecord::Base

  before_save :encrypt_password
  after_save :send_welcome_email
```

```
    private
    def encrypt_password
      # do work here...
    end

    def send_welcome_email
      # send_welcome_email
    end

  end
```

So now when you call the `save` method, it first checks to see if any registered call-backs should happen before the `save` action is invoked. In this case there is an `encrypt_password` callback, so it calls that method. Then it calls the actual `save` method that persists the record to the database. Then it checks to see if any callbacks are registered that need to be called after the record has been saved. Again, we have a registered callback that will send our welcome email.

Obviously this is an overly simple example, and I have left out a few things about how the underpinnings of ActiveRecord work, and that is because this isn't a book on ActiveRecord. But I find this to be a simple example of how callbacks work and why they can be helpful.

Implementing Callbacks

Now that you have a simple grasp on what callbacks are, we can start to look at how you can use callbacks with your distributed applications to make them more power-ful, and even more loosely coupled.

`Rinda` has three different events we can observe: `take`, `write`, and `delete`. The first two map directly to the `TupleSpace` methods we looked at in the section on `TupleSpaces`. For example, anytime someone takes a `Tuple` that matches our observed `Tuple` template, a notification is sent back to our observer to let us know. The same thing applies to `write`. The `delete` and `close` events are slightly differ-ent, and we will talk about those shortly.

Let's look at some code. Here we have a simple service that just serves up a number:

```
require 'rinda/ring'
DRb.start_service
ring_server = Rinda::RingFinger.primary
```

```
ring_server.write([:callback_service, 0], 30)

DRb.thread.join
```

There's nothing too special about our service. The only thing worth noting is that we are not using a `Rinda::SimpleRenewer` to handle the expiration of our `Tuple`. Instead, we have set it to 30 seconds. We will look at `Renewers` later in this chapter. We will also come back to the 30-second expiration in just a minute. First, let's look at our simple client:

```
require 'rinda/ring'

DRb.start_service
ring_server = Rinda::RingFinger.primary

service = ring_server.take([:callback_service, nil])

ring_server.write([:callback_service,
                    (service.last + 1)], 30)
```

All our client is doing is taking the `:callback_service` `Tuple` from the server, adding 1 to the number, and writing it back, again with a 30-second expiration.

To help debug our fantastic distributed application, we would like to know whenever someone takes a `Tuple` that matches `:callback_service`, whenever someone writes to the `:callback_service` `Tuple`, and when and if the `:callback_service` `Tuple` expires. Doing all of this is actually remarkably easy using the callback system built into `Rinda`. Let's look at how we would write a client to listen for these events:

```
require 'rinda/ring'

DRb.start_service
ring_server = Rinda::RingFinger.primary

service = ring_server.read([:callback_service, nil])

observers = []

observers << ring_server.notify('write',
                                [:callback_service, nil],
                                60)
```

```
observers << ring_server.notify('take',
                                [:callback_service, nil],
                                60)
observers << ring_server.notify('delete',
                                [:callback_service, nil],
                                60)

threads = []

observers.each do |observer|
  threads << Thread.new do
    observer.each do |event|
      puts event.inspect
    end
  end
end

threads.each {|t| t.join}
```

This code might seem a bit daunting at first, but actually it's fairly straightforward
and simple. Let's look at just a piece of it first:

```
ring_server.notify('write', [:callback_service, nil], 60)
```

All we are doing with this line of code is telling the RingServer to give us a
NotifyTemplateEntry object for the write action matching the Tuple template
[:callback_service, nil], and we want to stop listening after 60 seconds. If we
want to listen for callbacks indefinitely, we can either pass in nil for the last parameter or not pass in the parameter. I have chosen 60 seconds to demonstrate something
a little later. The NotifyTemplateEntry object we receive from the RingServer can
then be used to process our callback events.

In our code we are creating three different callbacks. The first two we have already
discussed and should be familiar to you by now. The third, however, is a fairly new
topic. We will discuss it a bit more in the section "Renewing Rinda Services," but what
we are doing with the delete callback is asking for a notification whenever a Tuple
has been explicitly deleted by another service or when the RingServer deletes the
Tuple because it has expired.

All that is left is to create a separate Thread for each of our observers and then
just call the each method on the observer and print the event we receive.

When our client runs, it takes out the `Tuple`, increments the number, and then writes the `Tuple` back to the `RingServer`:

```
["take", [:callback_service, 0]]
["write", [:callback_service, 1]]
```

As you can see, the event we receive from our callback is an `Array` containing two parameters. The first parameter is the type of notification we are receiving. For example, in our first event, we receive a `take` callback. The second parameter contains the actual `Tuple` that triggered the callback. This is useful if we want to do something such as logging the event, as we just did.

Thirty seconds after we receive our first callbacks, the `RingServer` automatically expires the `Tuple` so that the `delete` callback is triggered:

```
["delete", [:callback_service, 1]]
```

Another 30 seconds after that, our callbacks expire, and we receive a `close` notification for each of them:

```
["close"]
["close"]
["close"]
```

We have not previously mentioned the `close` callback, but its use should be fairly obvious. Because we specified that we want our callback hooks active for only 60 seconds when they expire, we get a callback telling us that. This event could then be used to do everything from shutting down the program to writing to a log to simply reregistering itself.

In Summary

This section was a brief introduction to the ideas and concepts behind callbacks and observers. We used those ideas and implement callbacks for a simple service, and you saw how each of them responded over time and what their response properties looked like.

If you would like to know more about the observer design pattern, and design patterns in general, I recommend that you read Russ Olsen's great book on design patterns, *Design Patterns in Ruby* (Addison-Wesley Professional, 2007). It is a wonderful book that is easy to read and follow along with; it should be required reading for every Ruby developer. The author does a wonderful job explaining the pattern in great detail, a subject that is much deeper than I have time to explain here.

Security with Rinda

In Chapter 1, when we discussed DRb, we talked about security. Because Rinda is built on top of the DRb libraries, we are already pretty much armed with all there is to know about security when using Rinda. Let's do a quick review of some of those points, and I'll point out where Rinda may differ slightly.

First, let's review this code sample again:

```
require 'drb'

# !!! UNSAFE CODE DO NOT RUN !!!
ro = DRbObject::new_with_uri("druby://your.server.com:8989")
class << ro
  undef :instance_eval
end
ro.instance_eval("`rm -rf *`")
```

If you remember, this block of code has the unfortunate side effect of deleting the entire file system on the server it gets executed on. This is still true. If you do not set your $SAFE level when using Rinda, your server *will be unsecure!* I cannot stress that point enough. Make sure you are at least running at $SAFE level 1. Please review the "Security" section of Chapter 1 if you still do not understand this point.

Access Control Lists (ACLs)

Our knowledge of ACLs serves us well in Rinda, because there is no change in how we do things in that area. In Rinda ACLs are even more useful than in straight DRb applications. In DRb you have to know exactly where the application you are looking for is. Using the premise of security through obscurity, you can say that only applications that you want to access the service will know where to find it. Of course, this is a bad idea for many reasons, but this book is not here to talk about network, or application, security at that level. All I will say on that subject is, please don't use this

method of security. Even a simple ACL will help safeguard your application, and it is
just a few extra lines of code.

If I haven't yet stressed the importance of ACLs enough, I'm about to stress them
even more when it comes to Rinda applications. Remember that Rinda applications
are self-discoverable. Each service starts and registers itself with the RingServer. The
RingServer then broadcasts across the network, telling anyone who will listen where
it is and what it has to offer. ACLs can help keep those pesky unwanted visitors from
using your service. Figure 2-3 shows the typical life cycle of a Rinda application
involving ACLs. The client queries the RingServer, asking where it can find a particular service. The RingServer responds with the service's address. The client then
sends a request to the service. The service allows or denies access to the client based
on the installed ACL.

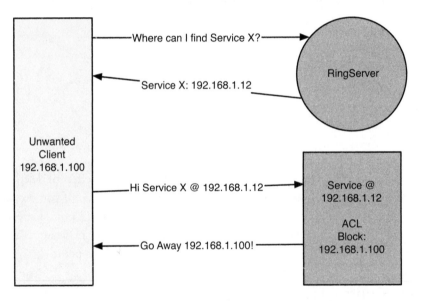

Figure 2-3   The typical life cycle of a Rinda application involving ACLs.

When you install an ACL on a service, this prevents unwanted[6] clients from
accessing the service. What it does not do is stop those unwanted clients from seeing
the service. It also does not stop an unwanted client from hitting the service and
potentially creating a denial-of-service attack on the server.

For the installed ACL to work, the client must first connect to the service. The service can then either accept or reject that request. Because of this, a malicious client could keep sending requests to the service, despite the service's rejecting the requests, thereby bringing down the service.

Unfortunately, we can't do anything about this problem from the level of our code. We can, however, be smart about our service architecture and network security to help prevent these sorts of attacks.

Using Rinda over SSL

Using Rinda over SSL is possible. It's not that different from what we have to do when setting up DRb to work over SSL. However, using Rinda over SSL has one small drawback: we lose the ability for Rinda to dynamically bind to any available port. This affects only the server code. The client still is completely unaware of where the service is and uses the RingServer to find the service's location.

In Chapter 1, when we talked about using DRb over SSL, we set up our "Hello World" application to be secure. Let's take that application and upgrade it to use Rinda. Normally we start with the server, but let's look at our client first for a change:

```
require 'drb'
require 'drb/ssl'
require 'rinda/ring'

config = {
  :SSLVerifyMode => OpenSSL::SSL::VERIFY_PEER,
  :SSLCACertificateFile => "CA/cacert.pem",
}

DRb.start_service(nil, nil, config)

ring_server = Rinda::RingFinger.primary

service = ring_server.read([:hello_world_service, nil])
server = service[1]

puts server.say_hello

puts service.inspect
```

With the exception of using `Rinda` to find the service, instead of hardcoding it with `DRb`, our client code doesn't look any different than it did when we set it up the first time to talk SSL to the server.

Now let's look at our server:

```ruby
require 'drb'
require 'drb/ssl'
require 'rinda/ring'

class HelloWorldServer
  include DRbUndumped

  def say_hello
    "Hello, world!"
  end

end

config = {
  :SSLPrivateKey =>
    OpenSSL::PKey::RSA.new(
      File.read("hello-server/hello-server_keypair.pem")
  ),
  :SSLCertificate =>
    OpenSSL::X509::Certificate.new(
        File.read("hello-server/cert_hello-server.pem")
    ),
}

DRb.start_service("drbssl://127.0.0.1:61677", nil, config)
ring_server = Rinda::RingFinger.primary
ring_server.write([:hello_world_service,
                    HelloWorldServer.new],
                   Rinda::SimpleRenewer.new)
DRb.thread.join
```

Again, the code doesn't look too different from the first time around, except that we are now using `Rinda` to announce the service. With that said, normally when we call the `start_service` method in a `Rinda` service, we don't call it with any parameters. This time, however, we are passing in three parameters: the host and port we want to bind the service to, `nil` because we won't share anything directly (we will use `Rinda` to manage our service), and a `Hash` configuration of our SSL options.

If you remember back in the "DRb Over SSL" section of Chapter 1, we saw that we had to tell the service to use the `drbssl` protocol. Well, the same here is true. That is why we had to pass in the host and port we wanted to bind to. Unfortunately, there is no way to just specify that we want to use the `drbssl` protocol without also having to bind our service to a specific host and port. This means that if we are to fire up two instances of our "Hello World" service, we must make sure that they are not stepping on each other's toes.

If we were to run this example, we would see that our client would output something along these lines:

```
Hello, world!
[:hello_world_service, #<DRb::DRbObject:0x33fa68 @ref=1712560,
@uri="drbssl://127.0.0.1:61677">]
```

So we can see that although we had to hardcode our server to a specific host and port, our client found that information dynamically by querying the `RingServer`.

Selecting a RingServer

Whenever we have discussed security, all we have really talked about is malicious clients trying to either attack our services or send dangerous or bogus messages to our servers. But what about the security of our clients? A hacker could just as easily set up a server that pretends to be a valid server and intercept requests from our clients. Certainly using things like SSL can help prevent this type of interception, because requests are terminated if either side of the relationship does not present the right credentials. The other option we have is to be more selective in choosing our `RingServer`.

Tip: Easing Development

If you are working in a development or testing environment that has more than one person working on `Rinda`-based applications, it is easy to accidentally select someone else's `RingServer` instead of your own. This can lead to chaos and confusion as you start overwriting someone else's `Tuples`, or they yours. Using either a firewall or the techniques discussed in this section will make your development experience less painful.

So far in all our examples we have somewhat magically been locating the `RingServer` we were hoping to find. We have been calling the following code:

```
ring_server = Rinda::RingFinger.primary
```

How has this code been finding our `RingServer`? Great question. Before we answer it, let's look at how we have been starting our `RingServer` so far:

```
Rinda::RingServer.new(Rinda::TupleSpace.new)
```

When we start our `RingServer` in this fashion, we are telling `Rinda` to start a `RingServer` and bind it to port 7647. When we call the `primary` method on `Rinda::RingFinger`, it first looks to see if somewhere on the local network a `RingServer` is broadcasting on port 7647. The first `RingServer` it finds broadcasting on that port is returned. If no `RingServer` is found broadcasting on the network, it then looks at the `localhost` of the requestor to see if a `RingServer` is broadcasting there. Again, if it is found, it is returned; otherwise, an `exception` is raised. This process is shown in Figure 2-4.

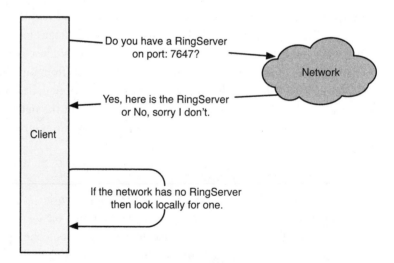

Figure 2-4 The "common" flow to look up a `RingServer` is to query the network for a `RingServer` on port 7647. If one is found, it is returned; otherwise, the `localhost` of the requestor is queried for the `RingServer`.

Now that you understand how the simple case of starting and locating a `RingServer` works, let's fire up a `RingServer` on a nonstandard port:

```
require 'rinda/ring'
require 'rinda/tuplespace'

DRb.start_service
Rinda::RingServer.new(Rinda::TupleSpace.new, 9000)
DRb.thread.join
```

The only change we make to our "normal" `RingServer` is to pass a different port to the new method on `Rinda::RingServer`. Now our server will start on port 9000.

If we were to try and find a `RingServer` now using our "normal" method of finding one:

```
require 'rinda/ring'

DRb.start_service
ring_server = Rinda::RingFinger.primary
```

we would get the following exception:

```
RuntimeError: RingNotFound
```

Obviously using the primary method on `Rinda::RingFinger` won't work, because it's looking for a `RingServer` broadcasting on port 7647. So how do we find it? Let's start by firing up a couple of `RingServers` so that we know when we have connected the correct one:

```
require 'rinda/ring'
require 'rinda/tuplespace'

DRb.start_service

[9000, 9001].each do |port|
  ts = Rinda::TupleSpace.new
  ts.write([:some_service, "#{Socket.gethostname}-port: #{port}"])
end

DRb.thread.join
```

Here we are starting up two `RingServers`. One is on port 9000, and the other is on port 9001. We have written a `Tuple` to each of their `TupleSpaces`, identifying which server we are talking to. This will make it easier for us in a minute to make sure the right `RingServer` is responding to us.

The first thing we have to do is create a new instance of `Rinda::RingFinger`. Now, if we were to create the instance as follows,

```
ring_finger = Rinda::RingFinger.new
```

we would not be doing anything different than what is happening under the covers when we call the `primary` class method. We will still only be looking for `RingServers` broadcasting on port 7647—first on the network, and then on the `localhost`.

The new method on `Rinda::RingFinger` takes two parameters. The first is an `Array`. This `Array` defaults to `['<broadcast>', 'localhost']`. These represent the hosts that we want to search for our `RingServers`. An `Array` is used to specify order, so be aware that the order in which you have your servers listed in the `Array` will be the order in which they are searched. If `nil` is passed in as the first argument, the list defaults to `['localhost']`. I don't know why it defaults to just `['local-host']` and not `['<broadcast>', 'localhost']`, but just be aware that it does. If we knew that our `RingServer` was hosted at `ringserver.example.com` on the default port of 7647, we would create a new `Rinda::RingFinger` like this:

```
ring_finger = Rinda::RingFinger.new(['ringserver.example.com'])
```

Getting back to our example, we have created two `RingServers` on ports 9000 and 9001, respectively. Let's try to find the one on port 9001:

```
require 'rinda/ring'

DRb.start_service

ring_finger = Rinda::RingFinger.new(['<broadcast>', 'localhost'],
                                    9001)
```

When creating our `Rinda::RingFinger`, we wanted to re-create the default lookup behavior, so we passed in the `Array` of `['<broadcast>', 'localhost']`. And since we wanted to look only on port 9001, we passed that in as the second parameter. That code should run and exit without any errors. The question still persists: How do we find a `RingServer`?

There are three ways we can find a `RingServer` once we have a properly config-ured `Rinda::RingFinger`. The first method is to use the `lookup_ring_any` method. This method is similar to the `primary` class method we are used to using. It finds the first `RingServer` that meets the specifications of the `Rinda::RingFinger` we created and returns that.

```
ring_finger.lookup_ring_any.read([:some_service, nil])
```

The next way of finding a `RingServer` is to use the `each` method. The `each` method will iterate through each of the `RingServers` it finds that matches the `Rinda::RingFinger` we created and yield up each `RingServer`:

```
ring_finger.each do |ring_server|
  ring_server.read([:some_service, nil])
end
```

The final way of finding a `RingServer` is to use the `primary` accessor method. This method has a major problem, however. Because `primary` is an accessor method, it is possible that it can return `nil` if it has not been set. You can either manually set the `primary` accessor yourself, or you can call either the `each` or `lookup_ring_any` method first, and it will set the `primary` accessor for you. The `lookup_ring_any` method determines what the primary `RingServer` should be set to by using the last `RingServer` found. So, by default, this is the one being served up by `localhost`. If we were to change our host `Array` to be `['<broadcast>']`, the primary `RingServer` would get set to the last server in the list. This is usually either the last alphabetically or the last by IP address. Because of this, I recommend not using the `primary` accessor, unless you are the one who is setting it.

```
require 'rinda/ring'

DRb.start_service

ring_finger = Rinda::RingFinger.new(['<broadcast>', 'localhost'],
                            9001)

puts ring_finger.primary.inspect

puts ring_finger.lookup_ring_any.read([:some_service, nil]).inspect
```

```
puts ring_finger.primary.read([:some_service, nil]).inspect

ring_finger.each do |ring_server|
  puts ring_server.inspect
  puts ring_server.read([:some_service, nil]).inspect
end
```

If we were to run this code, we would see something like this printed:

```
nil
[:some_service, "macbates.home-port: 9001"]
[:some_service, "macbates.home-port: 9001"]
#<DRb::DRbObject:0x3bddf0 @uri="druby://macbates.home:56482",
@ref=1854020>
[:some_service, "macbates.home-port: 9001"]
```

As you can see, the `primary` accessor is `nil` the first time we try to access it. After we call the `lookup_ring_any` method, the `primary` accessor is now set and returns the expected result.

We can demonstrate a lot of these points by running our multiple `RingServers` on two machines and running the following code on one of them:

```
require 'rinda/ring'

DRb.start_service

ring_finger = Rinda::RingFinger.new(['localhost', '<broadcast>'],
                                    9001)

ring_finger.lookup_ring_any

puts "primary: #{ring_finger.primary.inspect}\n\n"

sleep(5)

ring_finger.each do |ring_server|
  puts ring_server.inspect
  puts ring_server.read([:some_service, nil]).inspect
  puts "\n"
end
```

The result is something like this:

```
primary: #<DRb::DRbObject:0x3be070 @uri="druby://macbates.home:56482",
 @ref=1854020>

#<DRb::DRbObject:0x3be070 @uri="druby://macbates.home:56482",
@ref=1854020>
[:some_service, "macbates.home-port: 9001"]

#<DRb::DRbObject:0x3bd350 @uri="druby://macbates.home:56482",
@ref=1854020>
[:some_service, "macbates.home-port: 9001"]

#<DRb::DRbObject:0x3bb668 @uri="druby://biglaptop.home:53886",
@ref=1786160>
[:some_service, "biglaptop.home-port: 9001"]
```

The code was executed on a machine called "macbates." The RingServers were
started on "macbates" and "biglaptop." We can see that the RingServer found on
"macbates" was set to be the primary because we had localhost set as the last place
to look for RingServers. You'll notice that when we looped over each of the
RingServers, our Rinda::RingFinger actually found three RingServers, two of
them being the same instance of the one that resides on the "macbates" computer. The
reason is that our Rinda::RingFinger found the "macbates" RingServer twice. It
first found "macbates" when it searched the network, and then it found "macbates"
when it looked at the localhost. If we were to search only the network using the
['<broadcast>'] Array, we would have the "macbates" RingServer in our list
only once.

   If we were to call the to_a method on our Rinda::RingFinger instance, assuming we were searching only the network, and not our localhost, we would expect to
get back an Array that contains two entries—one for "biglaptop" and the other for
"macbates":

```
puts ring_finger.to_a.inspect
```

However, we actually get back the following:

```
[#<DRb::DRbObject:0x3bb668 @uri="druby://biglaptop.home:53886",
 @ref=1786160>]
```

What happened to the second entry? When the `lookup_ring_any` method is called and it generates the list of `RingServers`, it pops the last entry off the list and assigns it to the `primary` accessor. Therefore, that entry is no longer part of this list of found `RingServers`. The reason the author of this code gave for this choice is that the `to_a` method is supposed to return the rest of the `RingServers` found. To get a full list of all the `RingServers` found, you would have to combine the `primary` accessor and the return value of the `to_a` method. The `each` method gets around this by first yielding the `primary` accessor and then calling the `each` method on the `Array` returned by the `to_a` method and yielding those values. This can be a gotcha, so be sure to watch out for it.

In Summary

In this section we have reviewed some lessons we learned when we first spoke of DRb. We looked at those lessons and saw how to apply them to our `Rinda` applications. We also dug deeper into the innards of searching for `RingServers`. We found a few gotchas to watch out for and saw how to work around them.

Renewing Rinda Services

Back when we talked about writing `Tuples` to `TupleSpaces`, we briefly touched on the subject of `Renewers`. I said that, simply put, a `Renewer` determines how long the `Tuple` will live and when it gets expired. That is true, but as with most things, a few subtleties should be examined.

When we have created `Tuples`, we have created them with code that looks similar to the following:

```
ring_server.write([:some_service, 'some value'],
                   Rinda::SimpleRenewer.new)
```

We also could have written that same code as follows:

```
ring_server.write([:some_service, 'some value'], 180)
```

Both lines of code do the same thing. They tell the `RingServer` that this `Tuple` should expire 180 seconds after the last time it was touched. When someone goes to touch the `Tuple`, it is checked to see if it has expired. If the `Tuple` has expired, it checks with its `Renewer` to see if it should be renewed and, if so, for how long.

Using a Numeric to Renew a Service

Using a `Numeric` to represent the number of seconds a `Tuple` should live is the easiest way of setting an expiration. Let's look at a simple example:

```
require 'rinda/ring'

DRb.start_service
ring_server = Rinda::RingFinger.primary
ring_server.write([:count_service, 0], 10)

DRb.thread.join
```

With this code we are telling `Rinda` to expire the `Tuple` after 10 seconds. When using a `Numeric` for this value, we are also telling `Rinda` that we do not want this `Tuple` to self-renew. After 10 seconds this `Tuple` will be purged from the `TupleSpace`. Let's look at a client that demonstrates this:

```
require 'rinda/ring'
require 'timeout'

DRb.start_service
ring_server = Rinda::RingFinger.primary

6.times do
  Timeout.timeout(2) do
    puts ring_server.read([:count_service, nil]).inspect
  end
  sleep(1)
end

sleep(6)
Timeout.timeout(2) do
  puts ring_server.read([:count_service, nil]).inspect
end
```

Here we are looping six times, reading the `Tuple`, and sleeping for a second. Because we have a 10-second expiration time, this should not be a problem. Then we sleep for another 6 seconds and try again. When we do that, we are trying to access the `Tuple` at least 12 seconds after we have created it. The resulting output should look something like this:

```
[:count_service, 0]
[:count_service, 0]
[:count_service, 0]
[:count_service, 0]
[:count_service, 0]
[:count_service, 0]
Timeout::Error: execution expired
```

Using nil to Renew a Service

If we always want our `Tuples` to live forever, without fear of their expiring, using `nil` to set the expiration is the easiest way:

```
require 'rinda/ring'

DRb.start_service
ring_server = Rinda::RingFinger.primary
ring_server.write([:count_service, 0], nil)

DRb.thread.join
```

If we were to run our same client against this server again, we would see that the client never hits an exception, and we receive printouts for each `Tuple` successfully.

Using the SimpleRenewer Class

We have been using the `Rinda::SimpleRenewer` class throughout most of this chapter. By default this class sets a 180-second expiration time for the `Tuple`. When that expiration is reached, `Rinda` queries the `SimpleRenewer` to see if the `Tuple` should be renewed. The `SimpleRenewer` class tells `Rinda` to renew it again for another 180 seconds. You can change this period of time, 180 seconds, when you instantiate the class, like this:

```
Rinda::SimpleRenewer.new(10)
```

Now the `Rinda::SimpleRenewer` will set the `Tuple` to be renewed every 10 seconds. If you want infinite life, it is probably best to use `nil`, because this will have the least system impact. If you want something fancier, you need to write a custom `Renewer`.

Custom Renewers

Writing a custom `Renewer` is incredibly easy. Writing a custom `Renewer` has two main ingredients. The first is the `DRbUndumped` module. This ensures that the `Renewer` can be transported across the wire to the `RingServer`. The second ingredient is a `renew` method.

The `renew` method has to return one of three possible types—`nil`, `false`, or `Numeric`. Again, if you return `nil`, the `Tuple` lives for infinity. If you return `false`, Rinda expires the `Tuple` right then and there. Finally, if you return a `Numeric` value, Rinda checks the `renew` method again after that number of seconds.

Let's write a custom `Renewer` that lets the `Tuple` be renewed for only N times for X seconds at a time:

```ruby
class LimitedRenewer
  include DRbUndumped

  attr_accessor :ttl
  attr_accessor :limit
  attr_accessor :current_run

  def initialize(limit = 5, ttl = 2)
    self.limit = limit
    self.ttl = 2
    self.current_run = 0
  end

  def renew
    if self.current_run < self.limit
      self.current_run += 1
      puts "Will renew for #{self.ttl} seconds...
(#{self.current_run})"
      return self.ttl
    else
      puts 'No longer valid!'
```

```
        return false
    end
  end

end
```

In our `renew` method we check to see if the `current_run` is less than the imposed limit. If it is, we can renew the `Tuple` again for the given `ttl` (time to live). We increment the `current_run` so that we will eventually hit our limit. If our `current_run` is equal to or greater than the limit, we return `false`, and the `Tuple` expires.

Our client in this example just keeps looping and reading the `Tuple` until it has expired:

```
require 'rinda/ring'
require 'timeout'

DRb.start_service
ring_server = Rinda::RingFinger.primary

loop do
  Timeout.timeout(2) do
    puts ring_server.read([:count_service, nil]).inspect
  end
  sleep(1)
end
```

When we run this on the server side, we should see the following printed:

```
Will renew for 2 seconds... (1)
Will renew for 2 seconds... (2)
Will renew for 2 seconds... (3)
Will renew for 2 seconds... (4)
Will renew for 2 seconds... (5)
No longer valid!
```

On the client side we will eventually be thrown a `Timeout::Error` exception.

One disadvantage of the `Renewer` system is that the `Renewer` class does not have access to the `Tuple` it is renewing. Because of this, it is impossible to decide the fate of the `Tuple` based on the `Tuple`'s contents. Again, this is just another thing to watch out for when you're developing a `Rinda` application.

In Summary

In this section we dove into the depths of how the life cycle of a `Tuple` is decided. We looked at how to make a `Tuple` last for only a certain amount of time, how to make it live forever, and how to make it do something in between.

Understanding how long a `Tuple` lives is vital to building a properly functioning application. If you set the wrong value, or type, to determine the life of a `Tuple`, you risk having your applications not function properly, or worse, not function at all.

Conclusion

In this chapter we have taken a deep dive into all that `Rinda` has to offer. We demystified how `Rinda` implements the Linda distributed computing paradigm. `Rinda` is a powerful, easy-to-use, and sometimes dangerous platform that is offered to Ruby developers. We have looked at what makes it so powerful, and we have learned where the dangers and pitfalls await us.

We've explored creating, discovering, and securing our `RingServers` and services. You now understand how `TupleSpaces` work. You know how to query them, retrieve them, write them, and delete them. You also now know how to trigger callbacks when an event occurs on a `Tuple`.

Combined with what you learned in Chapter 1 about `DRb`, you now have a full understanding of what is bundled in the standard Ruby library. All that we have covered is applicable to both Ruby 1.8.x and Ruby 1.9.x.

Part II, "Third-Party Frameworks and Libraries," of this book explores third-party frameworks and tools that you can use when writing your distributed applications. Before you read about those tools and frameworks, I encourage you to spend some time with what is available to you in the standard library in the form of `DRb` and `Rinda`. A lot of the third-party projects you will work on use these libraries under the covers, so it would behoove you to fully understand the foundation. We have covered a lot of that foundation in the first two chapters, but no amount of reading can replace real-world experience.

So experiment a bit. Use these first two chapters as a guide during your experiments. When you're ready, we can continue on our journey of distributed programming with Ruby.

Endnotes

1. http://en.wikipedia.org/wiki/Linda_(coordination_language)

2. http://en.wikipedia.org/wiki/User_Datagram_Protocol

3. http://en.wikipedia.org/wiki/Tuple_space

4. http://en.wikipedia.org/wiki/Tuple

5. http://en.wikipedia.org/wiki/Year_2038_problem

6. I use the term "unwanted" here loosely. Because ACLs in DRb are based on IP address, it is impossible to have two clients sitting on the same IP address and to block one while allowing the other. You would have to do that programmatically in your code.

PART II
Third-Party Frameworks and Libraries

Part I of this book delved deeply into what the Ruby standard library ships with, in terms of distributed programming, and how we can use that to build our distributed applications. Part II covers third-party frameworks and libraries that are available to either augment or replace DRb and Rinda.

Some of these tools offer a similar approach to what we are used to with DRb and Rinda, and others offer a radically different approach to distributed programming. We'll talk about each package's strengths and weaknesses, as well as when and where you might want to implement the library.

To give our discussions some context, we will first create our now-standard "Hello World" and "Distributed Logger" programs. In some cases the tool won't quite lend itself to these examples, and that's okay. That is all part of the evaluation process. We need to see how each tool handles the same task. From there we will learn if it's appropriate for that task. Finally, we will move onto a project or two that showcases the uniqueness of the tool being discussed.

It's important to note that just because a project makes it into our discussion in this part of the book doesn't mean that it is the best tool, but rather that it has made some impact or represents a unique approach to the problem at hand. Other frameworks and libraries also didn't make the cut. This doesn't mean that those libraries are not valid or good. It just means that this book has limited space, and some decisions had to be made, or that those libraries were already duplicating important patterns and discussions that were already discussed.

Finally, please keep in mind that this part of the book is not meant to be a comprehensive manual for these libraries. You should use this part as a jumping-off point for your own discoveries. When you encounter a challenge in writing your distributed application, flip through the forthcoming chapters and see if one of the tools highlighted might help you. Then build the projects we discuss, look at the library's source code, join a mailing list for it, Google it, or whatever other way you use to learn about something.

CHAPTER 3
RingyDingy

"A little boat that keeps your DRb service afloat!" That is how developer Eric Hodel describes his RingyDingy gem at http://seattlerb.rubyforge.org/RingyDingy/. In Chapter 2, "Rinda," we discussed `RingServers`, including how to build a simple one. RingyDingy aims to make the process of managing a `RingServer` a little easier and a little less prone to some of the issues that can sometimes occur with `RingServers`.

Installation

RingyDingy is installed using RubyGems:

```
$ gem install RingyDingy
```

It is important that you use correct capitalization. If you do not, RubyGems will not be able to find the gem and install it correctly. Upon installation, you should see the following message:

```
Successfully installed RingyDingy-1.2.1
```

Getting Started with RingyDingy

When you install the RingyDingy gem, it installs a binary for you called `ring_server`. This binary, probably not surprisingly, runs a `RingServer` for you. Let's take a quick look at what options are available on this binary:

```
$ ring_server --help
```

This should print something similar to the following:

```
Usage: RingyDingy::RingServer [options]
Run, find, or modify the behavior of a Rinda::RingServer.
With no arguments a Rinda::RingServer is started and runs in
   the foreground.
RingServer options:
    -d, --daemon                Run a RingServer as a daemon
    -v, --verbose               Enable verbose mode
Miscellaneous options:
    -l, --list                  List services on available RingServers
        --set-verbose=BOOLEAN   Enable or disable verbose mode
                                on available RingServers
                                (except daemon RingServers)
```

The two most important flags for us are --d and --v. The --d flag, as stated in the description, runs the `RingServer` as a daemon in the background. You should run with this command in production. However, because we are learning about RingyDingy, we can simply run it in the foreground so that we can keep an eye on its output. To help with that, we should use the --v flag when we start the `RingServer` in our development environment. That will increase the amount of logging to the screen, so we can more easily debug any issues we may come across. Let's start our RingyDingy `RingServer` now with the following command:

```
$ ring_server --v
```

You should get output similar to the following:

```
registration and expiration logging enabled
listening on druby://macbates.home:50823
```

Obviously your computer name and port will be different, but you get the idea. That's all we need to do to get RingyDingy up and running.

"Hello World" the RingyDingy Way

With our RingyDingy `RingServer` running and outputting useful logging information, we can now start our "Hello World" application. Fortunately we can make use of the code we wrote in Chapter 2 to power this chapter. Our server code for the `Rinda` "Hello World" application remains largely unchanged to use with RingyDingy:

```
require 'rinda/ring'

class HelloWorldServer
  include DRbUndumped

  def say_hello
    "Hello, world!"
  end

end

DRb.start_service
ring_server = Rinda::RingFinger.primary
ring_server.write([:name, :HelloWorldServer,
                  HelloWorldServer.new, 'I like to say hi!'],
                Rinda::SimpleRenewer.new)

DRb.thread.join
```

In fact, there is only one difference between the `Rinda` version and the Ringy-Dingy version of this code. Did you spot it? Don't worry if you didn't; it's a subtle change in the code. When we create our `Tuple` with RingyDingy, the library dictates that we use the following format:

```
[:name, <service_name>, <instance>, <description>]
```

Notice that the first parameter of the `Tuple` is hardcoded to the value `:name`. In our original "Hello World" application, we set that parameter to `:hello_world_ service`. Not a big change but a change nonetheless. The reason for this is simply

that the RingyDingy library has :name hardcoded in it. Why is that? No reason that
I can ascertain; it just is what it is. It is important, if you want to use RingyDingy
without altering its source code, that you use this Tuple pattern; otherwise, it won't
work for you.

When we run our "Hello World" server, we should see output similar to the following for our RingyDingy RingServer:

```
registered :HelloWorldServer, "I like to say hi!"
      URI: druby://192.168.1.12:52042 ref: 1961110
```

As with our server, we also have to update our client to use the preferred Ringy-
Dingy Tuple pattern:

```
require 'rinda/ring'

DRb.start_service
ring_server = Rinda::RingFinger.primary

service = ring_server.read([:name, nil, nil, nil])
server = service[2]

puts server.say_hello

puts service.inspect
```

When we run our client, we should see something like the following:

```
Hello, world!
[:name, :HelloWorldServer, #<DRb::DRbObject:0x3bb974 @ref=1961110,
 @uri="druby://192.168.1.12:52042">, "I like to say hi!"]
```

Building a Distributed Logger with RingyDingy

RingyDingy allows us to DRY up our server code a bit. We no longer have to remember a whole lot of messy Rinda API calls. Instead, we can wrap it up with a line or
two of RingyDingy code. Let's look at our "Distributed Logger" application to see
how we can make it more DRY.

If we were to write our "Distributed Logger" with `Rinda`, it would look something like the following:

```
require 'rinda/ring'
require 'logger'

DRb.start_service
ring_server = Rinda::RingFinger.primary
ring_server.write([:my_logger, :Logger,
                Logger.new(STDOUT), 'I like to log!'],
                Rinda::SimpleRenewer.new)

DRb.thread.join
```

With RingyDingy we can rewrite our logging server to look more like this:

```
require 'rubygems'
require 'ringy_dingy'
require 'logger'

RingyDingy.new(Logger.new(STDOUT), :MyRingyDingyLogger).run

DRb.thread.join
```

This is definitely a little cleaner and easier to follow. The first parameter to the `new` method on the `RingyDingy` class is the instance of the class we want to serve. The second parameter, which is optional, is the name we want to give the service. This defaults to `:RingyDingy` if we don't specify it. I prefer to specify it all the time, because it ensures that we don't have any naming conflicts. It is also more descriptive of the service if we do. It would be a nice enhancement to RingyDingy if it did some inspection on the instance and used the class name as the default name of the service; at the time of writing, however, this isn't the case.

Unfortunately, RingyDingy doesn't give us any nice ways to clean up our client code, so we have to stay with the traditional `Rinda` code we are now used to:

```
require 'rinda/ring'

DRb.start_service
ring_server = Rinda::RingFinger.primary
```

```
service = ring_server.read([:name, :MyRingyDingyLogger, nil, nil])
logger = service[2]

puts service.inspect

logger.info 'Hi There!
```

When we fire up our server, we should see a rough equivalent of the following:

```
registration and expiration logging enabled
listening on druby://macbates.home:52132
registered :MyRingyDingyLogger, "macbates.home_50587"
  URI: druby://macbates.home:52186 ref: 9073620
```

When we run our client, we should see the following on the client side:

```
[:name, :MyRingyDingyLogger, #<DRb::DRbObject:0x3bb938 @ref=9073620,
 @uri="druby://macbates.home:52186">, "macbates.home_50587"]
```

On the server side, we should see the following:

```
I, [2009-04-29T23:22:58.361040 #50587]  INFO -- : Hi There!
```

Letting RingyDingy Shine

RingyDingy offers a few other nice bits and pieces. One of the better features that the RingyDingy `ring_server` binary gives you for free is the ability to list available services. Assuming we had both our "Hello World" and "Distributed Logger" services registered with RingyDingy, and we ran the following command:

```
$ ring_server -l
```

we could expect to see something similar to the following returned:

```
Services on druby://macbates.home:52132
    :HelloWorldServer, "I like to say hi!"
        URI: druby://192.168.1.12:52761 ref: 1961150

    :MyRingyDingyLogger, "macbates.home_50587"
        URI: druby://macbates.home:52186 ref: 9073620
```

This is a great debugging tool. It makes troubleshooting much easier when you know what services are and aren't available, and where those services are actually located.

We can also gain access to this same information programmatically. Let's take a look at a quick example:

```
require 'rubygems'
require 'ringy_dingy/ring_server'

service_list = RingyDingy::RingServer.list_services

service_list.each do |host, services|
  puts "Host: #{host}"
  services.each do |service|
    puts "\t#{service.inspect}"
  end
end
```

In this code example we require the ringy_dingy/ring_server file. Then we call the list_services method on the RingyDingy::RingServer class, which returns to us a Hash of services.

Why do we get back a Hash and not an Array? The answer is because the key in the Hash is the host that is hosting the services, and the value is an Array of the services on that host. This is very helpful for diagnosing issues on a particular host.

After we get the Hash of services, we loop through each of keys, print the host, and then loop through each of the services for that host and print them. The results should look something like this:

```
Host: druby://macbates.home:52132
  [:name, :MyRingyDingyLogger, #<DRb::DRbObject:0x10aec08
@uri="druby://macbates.home:52186", @ref=9073620>,
"macbates.home_50587"]
  [:name, :HelloWorldServer, #<DRb::DRbObject:0x10aea50
@uri="druby://192.168.1.12:52761", @ref=1961150>, "I like to say hi!"]
```

Although this isn't the most helpful output, you get the idea that this sort of information can be very helpful, and with RingyDingy it is fairly easy to retrieve. You can, of course, write your own method to retrieve the list of services for a custom RingServer as well, but using RingyDingy means you don't have to.

Conclusion

Eric Hodel did a great job with this little library. The library doesn't try to be anything it is not. It just tries to make using `Rinda` and `RingServers` a little easier, and it does that nicely. My only complaint is the use of the hardcoded `:name` parameter in the `Tuple` template, but that is a small nuisance. It also would've been nice to get some help cleaning up the client side of things. I would love to do the following in my client:

```
RingyDingy.find(:MyRingyDingyLogger)
```

That would definitely DRY up my client code. Perhaps Eric will find it in his heart to update the library to do that.

In the documentation, RingyDingy mentions the following:

> *If communication between the RingServer and the RingyDingy is lost, RingyDingy will re-register its service with the RingServer when it reappears.*
>
> *Similarly, the RingServer will automatically drop registrations by a RingyDingy that it can't communicate with after a short timeout.*

I think I understand what Eric means by all that. However, that is as deep as the documentation goes on the subject. I have not been able to test what I think he means, so I won't make any grand promises about what the library can and cannot do in regards to expiring/renewing registrations.

Considering its relative ease of use, if you are doing straight-up `Rinda` applications, dropping RingyDingy into the mix is easy, and it will help you manage your applications a little easier.

CHAPTER 4

Starfish

Starfish[1] bills itself as "a utility to make distributed programming ridiculously easy." I think that is a bit of an overstatement, but Starfish certainly can make distributed programming easier. The library was built by Lucas Carlson of the website http://mog.com, who also co-wrote *Ruby Cookbook* (O'Reilly Media, Inc., 2006).[2]

Starfish sets out to fulfill two different, but useful, roles in the distributed programming world. In its first role Starfish sets out to play the part of a facilitator, setting up quick servers and clients that can be used to call and execute distributed code. In its second role Starfish implements a Ruby version of the popular MapReduce[3] distributed computing paradigm.

This chapter first looks at how to use Starfish to facilitate communication between distributed programs. Then you'll find out more about how we can use it to write MapReduce functions.

Installation

Starfish was built on DRb and Rinda as well as Lucas's own MapReduce library. To install Starfish we can use RubyGems:

```
$ gem install starfish
```

You may have to run this command with root privileges, depending on your environment. After installation you should see a message similar to the following:

```
Successfully installed starfish-1.2.1
```

Getting Started with Starfish

The documentation for Starfish gives a simple piece of sample code to get us into the flow of the library:

```
class Foo
  attr_reader :i

  def initialize
    @i = 0
  end

  def inc
    logger.info "YAY it incremented by 1 up to #{@i}"
    @i += 1
  end
end

server :log => "/tmp/foo.log" do |object|
  object = Foo.new
end

client do |object|
  object.inc
end
```

The documentation then tells us to run this code using the starfish binary. So assuming that we saved this file using the rather original filename of foo.rb, we would execute this code like this:

```
starfish foo.rb
```

At this point you see something like the following printed on the screen:

```
server started for #<Foo:0x184e774 @i=0>
```

After that you will see nothing. I recommend killing the process quickly so that you don't fill up your hard drive. If we examine the code, we see that the inc method on the Foo class is writing to the log file we created at /tmp/foo.log. That is why we didn't see anything print to the screen after we executed our file. Looking at our log file, we should see something like the following:

```
# Logfile created on Sat Apr 11 22:07:27 -0400 2009 by /
YAY it incremented by 1 up to 0
YAY it incremented by 1 up to 1
...
YAY it incremented by 1 up to 18837
YAY it incremented by 1 up to 18838
```

It's good to know that the library works. Now let's take a closer look at how it works, and then we'll try to make it do a few interesting things:

```
server :log => "/tmp/foo.log" do |object|
  object = Foo.new
end

client do |object|
  object.inc
end
```

The magic `server` and `client` methods appear courtesy of the `starfish` binary (more on that in a minute). Each of these methods takes a `Hash` of options. As you see with the call to the `server` method, we are telling it where to write the log file. The other parameter these methods take is a `block`. It is this `block` that forms the basis of the implementation of our server and clients.

In the case of the `server` method the `block` yields an `Object`. This `Object` needs to be set to the instance of whatever object you want to set up. As we talked about in Chapter 2, "Rinda," you can serve up only instances of `Objects`, not a pointer to the `Class` itself. With the `client` method we are yielded the instance of the `Object` we set up in the server method.

One quick point that I think is important to note, and you may have already figured this out by the log file, is that the `block` you use for the client will be run forever. It is called within an infinite loop and stops only if you raise an exception or exit the system. This is definitely something to be wary of. The client would run forever and keep asking the server if it had any messages that needed attention. If messages are found, the client processes them and then asks for more. We'll see a better example of this later in the chapter.

"Hello World" the Starfish Way

Let's look at how we can implement our standard "Hello World" application using Starfish. We'll start with writing it using the starfish binary that comes bundled with the gem. Then we'll look at what we would need to do to get the same application to work without the help of the binary.

Using the Starfish Binary

In the brief example that comes with Starfish, we saw the server and client both written in the same file. Although that is great in a sample file, in real life we would most likely want to have those in two separate files, potentially even running on different machines. So let's first look at what we would want our server file to look like:

```
class HelloWorld

  def say_hi
    'Hi There!'
  end

end

server do |object|
  object = HelloWorld.new
end
```

As you can see, our "Hello World" server is not that much different from the sample code that ships with Starfish. We have a HelloWorld class, and in our server block we create a new instance of that HelloWorld class and assign it to the object yielded by the server block. Assuming that this was in a file called server.rb, we would run it from the Terminal window like this:

```
starfish server.rb
```

However, when we run this, we receive the following error:

```
You must specify a client
```

To fix this error we have to modify our `server` slightly:

```
class HelloWorld

  def say_hi
    'Hi There!'
  end

end

server do |object|
  object = HelloWorld.new
end

# If we don't specify a dummy client we get the following error:
# You must specify a client
client {}
```

Notice that we added `client {}` to the bottom of the server file. The reason for this appears to be a bug or flaw in the Starfish architecture. Starfish expects to see both a server and a client declared in the same file when it is run with the `starfish` binary. It is easy enough to work around, but, as you'll see shortly, a few workarounds must be carried out, making Starfish a less-than-stellar way to accomplish the task at hand. But it does have its benefits, which is why we are going to keep pushing on.

Now when we run this, we should see the following output:

```
server started for #<HelloWorld:0x184a764>
```

Now we can turn our attention to the client for our "Hello World" application:

```
client do |hello_world|
  puts hello_world.say_hi
  exit(0)
end
```

Now we can run this as follows:

```
starfish client.rb
```

What happens when we run this? We see an oddly familiar, yet different, error message:

```
You must specify a server
```

We saw something similar earlier with our server. All we should need to do is add server {} to our client, and we should be all set. Right? Well, let's see what happens if we add that bit of code and rerun our client:

```
server started for nil
./client.rb:5: undefined method 'say_hi' for nil:NilClass
(NoMethodError)
```

Oops! That certainly didn't have the outcome we expected. In fact, it seemed to make matters worse. This appears to be one of the biggest quirks with Starfish. When you use the binary it comes with, it names the "server" after the filename. So, in our example the server that is hosting our "Hello World" application is named server.rb, because that's what the file it was started on was called. Because our client is called client.rb, it is searching for a server with that name, which doesn't exist.

So how do we solve this problem? Well, we can rename client.rb to server.rb, but most file systems, at least the ones I know of, don't like to have two files in the same location named the same thing. Plus, it would be weird to have a "client" named server.rb. We'll just have to find a better way.

Here's how we fix it:

```ruby
# If we don't put this here, Starfish will
# attempt to look for a server named after the
# current file. Since the name of the client file
# is different from the server file, we have to
# fool Starfish into believing it's running the
# server file. Without this we will receive the
# following error:
# You must specify a server
ARGV.unshift('server.rb')

client do |hello_world|
  puts hello_world.say_hi
  exit(0)
end
```

To solve the problem, we need to trick the `starfish` binary into thinking it is running a file called `server.rb`. That's why we added the following line:

```
ARGV.unshift('server.rb')
```

This is certainly not the most elegant solution, but it definitely gets the job done. We can confirm this by running the file. We should get the following:

```
Hi There!
```

Well, that is definitely better. Although still not great, it is definitely better in that it actually runs and gives us our desire output.

Saying Goodbye to the Starfish Binary

Although using the `starfish` binary is great for these examples, we might want to embed these servers and clients into a standard Ruby client. So how would we go about doing that? Well, let's start by seeing what happens when we run our "Hello World" server using the standard `ruby` binary:

```
ruby server.rb
```

We get the following exception:

```
server.rb:9: undefined method 'server' for main:Object (NoMethodError)
```

This isn't terribly surprising, because at the very least we need to include the Starfish libraries. So let's add the following to the top of our server.rb file:

```
require 'rubygems'
require 'starfish'
```

Now when we run it, we get an error similar to the following:

```
/usr/local/lib/ruby/gems/1.8/gems/starfish-1.2.1/lib/starfish.rb:32:in
  'basename': can't convert nil into String (TypeError)
       from /usr/local/lib/ruby/gems/1.8/gems/starfish-
1.2.1/lib/starfish.rb:32
       from
/usr/local/lib/ruby/site_ruby/1.8/rubygems/custom_require.rb:36:in
```

```
'gem_original_require'
    from
/usr/local/lib/ruby/site_ruby/1.8/rubygems/custom_require.rb:36:in
'require'
    from server.rb:2
```

So what is going on here? Well, it appears to be another decision made in the Starfish architecture. When we require `starfish`, it executes the following code:

```
@@options = {
    :log => "#{Dir.tmpdir}/#{File.basename(ARGV.first)}.log"
  }
```

As you can see, it is trying to get the `basename` of the first argument passed into the binary. This works great when you are using the `starfish` binary, because it is the receiver of the `ARGV` list. However, because we are using the `ruby` binary, we don't have access to that information.

So how do we fix this? We fix it in a similar way to how we fixed the error we were getting with our "client" earlier. Before our `require` statements, we need to add the following line:

```
ARGV.unshift('server.rb')
```

Again, this fools Starfish into thinking it is running from a file called `server.rb`. Now let's try to run our "server" again:

```
server.rb:13: undefined method 'server' for main:Object (NoMethodError)
```

Now we're back to the error we had earlier when we started trying to run our "server" without the `starfish` binary. Why is that? The reason is simple. When we use the `starfish` binary, it creates a `server` and `client` method on `Kernel`, which is how we can use these methods without error. However, since we are not using the binary, we have to alter our "server" a little more:

```
# If we don't make sure there is at least 1
# thing in the ARGV array an Exception will be raised!
# This has to happen before we require 'starfish'
ARGV.unshift('server.rb')
```

```
require 'rubygems'
require 'starfish'

class HelloWorld

  def say_hi
    'Hi There!'
  end

end

Starfish.server = lambda do |object|
  object = HelloWorld.new
end

Starfish.new('hello_world').server
```

Because we no longer have access to a `server` method on `Kernel`, we need to call it from the `Starfish` class directly and assign it a `lambda` to use for the "server."

After we create our server `lambda`, we can start the server itself with this line:

```
Starfish.new('hello_world').server
```

When we run this, we should see output similar to the following:

```
server started for #<HelloWorld:0x18a3da0>
```

Hooray! The server is now functioning without error. Notice that we didn't have to add the `client {}` to the bottom of the file. This is because we are not using the `starfish` binary, which was trying to run the "client" as well as the "server."

What about the client? Again, if we try to run our existing client, we get the following error:

```
client.rb:11: undefined method 'client' for main:Object
(NoMethodError)
```

By now you should understand why that is, so let's fix it:

```
# If we don't make sure there is at least 1
# thing in the ARGV array an Exception will be raised!
# This has to happen before we require 'starfish'
```

```
ARGV.unshift('server.rb')

require 'rubygems'
require 'starfish'

Starfish.client = lambda do | hello_world|
  puts hello_world.say_hi
  exit(0)
end

Starfish.new('hello_world').client
```

The changes we've made aren't that different from the ones we've made to our server. Now we should be able to run this and get the following:

```
Hi There!
```

Great! Now we know how to get a Starfish server and client running independently of the starfish binary. It is a bit troublesome, and these hacks could be fixed quite simply in the code base, but they are certainly not insurmountable.

Building a Distributed Logger with Starfish

Now that you have a basic understanding of Starfish, and how to run it using independent files, let's take a look at how we can build a distributed logger with the library. This will be a little trickier than you are used to, due to the Starfish architecture. As noted earlier, Starfish runs both the server and the client in infinite loops. This is fine for the server, because we want it to pick up any logging messages we may have, but we certainly can't run our client in one big infinite loop just so that we have access to the distributed logger object.

So how will we get around the design of Starfish to allow us to retrieve the distributed Logger object and use it outside of the block? It's actually not all that difficult. First, let's look at our server:

```
# If we don't make sure there is at least 1
# thing in the ARGV array an Exception will be raised!
# This has to happen before we require 'starfish'
ARGV.unshift('server.rb')
```

```
require 'rubygems'
require 'starfish'
require 'logger'

Starfish.server = lambda { |object|
  object = Logger.new(STDOUT)
}

Starfish.new('distributed_logger').server
```

Nothing is new here that we haven't seen in our previous examples with the "Hello World" application. The only real difference is that we are serving up a Logger instance instead of a HelloWorld instance. Now our client proves more difficult. Here is what we want the client code to look like:

```
# If we don't make sure there is at least 1
# thing in the ARGV array an Exception will be raised!
# This has to happen before we require 'starfish'
ARGV.unshift('client.rb')

require 'rubygems'
require 'starfish'

local_logger = nil
Starfish.client = lambda { |logger|
  local_logger = logger
  logger.info 'hi mr. distributed logger'
}
Starfish.new('distributed_logger').client
local_logger.info 'bye bye'
```

The problem is that, when we run this, we get an infinite printout that looks like this:

```
hi mr. distributed logger
hi mr. distributed logger
...
hi mr. distributed logger
hi mr. distributed logger
```

Notice that we don't see "bye bye" anywhere in there. The good news is we are not far from where we need to be. Let's look at how we can fix this code to get the desired results:

```ruby
# If we don't make sure there is at least 1
# thing in the ARGV array an Exception will be raised!
# This has to happen before we require 'starfish'
ARGV.unshift('client.rb')

require 'rubygems'
require 'starfish'

local_logger = nil
catch(:halt) do
  Starfish.client = lambda { |logger|
    local_logger = logger
    logger.info 'hi mr. distributed logger'
    throw :halt
  }
  Starfish.new('distributed_logger').client
end

local_logger.info 'bye bye'
```

The large difference in this code example from the previous example is the use of the Ruby throw/catch syntax. First we wrap our Starfish code in a catch block. It's important that we also wrap this line:

```ruby
Starfish.new('distributed_logger').client
```

If we had just wrapped the lambda that we send to the client class method, this would not work. When we create a new instance of the Starfish class and call the client method on it, that is what runs the lambda we passed in, and that is what eventually calls the throw directive.

Finally, in the lambda we call throw :halt. When the lambda is run, it sets the local variable local_logger to the distributed Logger instance, calls the info method on it with a message, and then calls the throw. Our catch block gracefully handles the throw and lets our application move on to call the info method on the local variable local_logger and send it the message "bye bye."

Now when we run this code we should get the following output on our server:

```
hi mr. distributed logger
bye bye
```

Again, a few more hacks to make this all work, but again, they are not insurmountable—just unfortunate.

Letting Starfish Shine

So far we have looked at how Starfish works. We've talked a lot about its weaknesses, but we haven't given the library a real chance to shine, so let's do just that.

To me, Starfish really excels as a means to do distributed queuing services. By no means is it the only one of its kind in this area, or even in this book, but it certainly is one of the easier systems to use.

In this example we will create a server that serves up tasks for the client to process. Sometimes there will be tasks, and sometimes there won't be. Sometimes there might be n tasks, and sometimes there will be just one.

In the real world these tasks would most likely be fed from a database, the file system, or some other location. In our simple example we will feed the server by creating task files in a specific directory. The server then will serve them to the client. The client will first process the task and then complete the task.

Let's see what our server will look like:

```
# If we don't make sure there is at least 1
# thing in the ARGV array an Exception will be raised!
# This has to happen before we require 'starfish'
ARGV.unshift('server.rb')

require 'rubygems'
require 'starfish'
require 'fileutils'

class TaskServer

  def each(&block)
    Dir.glob(File.join(File.dirname(__FILE__),
                       'tasks', '*.task')).each do |file_path|
      yield Task.new(file_path)
```

```
      end
    end

  end

class Task
  include DRbUndumped

  attr_accessor :file_path

  def initialize(file_path)
    self.file_path = file_path
  end

  def process
    File.read(file_path)
  end

  def complete
    FileUtils.rm_f(file_path)
  end

end

Starfish.server = lambda { |object|
  object = TaskServer.new
}

Starfish.new('task_server').server
```

First we create our `TaskServer` class. This class contains just one method, `each`. The each method looks in a directory called tasks that is on the same level as the file we are running. In that directory it finds all the *.task files. If it finds any files, it loops through them, creates a new `Task` instance, gives it the path to the .task file, and then yields that new `Task` instance.

Our `Task` class is defined next. Again, this class is quite simple. It takes one parameter on initialization, which is the path to the .task file. It then defines `process` and `complete` methods. In the `process` method we read the file and return its contents. In the `complete` method we delete the .task file from the system so that we don't accidentally process it again.

It is important to note that the `Task` class includes `DRbUndumped`. If we didn't include `DRbUndumped` into the `Task` class, we would get the following error:

```
NoMethodError: undefined method 'process' for
  #<DRb::DRbUnknown:0x183ce70>
```

You'll remember from our discussion of this subject in Chapter 1, "Distributed Ruby (DRb)," in the section "Proprietary Ruby Objects," that we can't send a proprietary class definition across the wire, unless we are sure that the client also has that same class definition available to it. If the "client" already had the `Task` defined, we wouldn't get this error. Because it does not, we have to access the `Task` class by reference instead of by value.

Now let's look at our client:

```
# If we don't make sure there is at least 1
# thing in the ARGV array an Exception will be raised!
# This has to happen before we require 'starfish'
ARGV.unshift('client.rb')

require 'rubygems'
require 'starfish'

Starfish.client = lambda do |tasks|
  tasks.each do |task|
    puts task.process
    task.complete
  end
  puts "sleeping..."
  sleep(1)
end

Starfish.new('task_server').client
```

Our client asks the server for any tasks it might have. It then iterates over those tasks, calls the `process` method, printing its output to the screen, and then calls the `complete` method. When the client is finished processing the tasks, it sleeps for a second before starting the cycle again.

Here is a simple script that populates tasks for you to test this:

```
i = 1
loop do
  path = File.join(File.dirname(__FILE__), 'tasks', "#{i}.task")
  File.open(path, 'w') {|f| f.write("I am task ##{i}")}
  i += 1
  sleep(rand)
end
```

If we fire up the server, client, and script to create some tasks, we should see output similar to the following printed on our client's screen:

```
sleeping...
I am task #1
sleeping...
I am task #2
I am task #3
I am task #4
sleeping...
I am task #5
I am task #6
sleeping...
I am task #7
sleeping...
I am task #8
I am task #9
sleeping...
I am task #10
I am task #11
sleeping...
I am task #12
I am task #13
I am task #14
sleeping...
I am task #15
I am task #16
I am task #17
sleeping...
I am task #18
sleeping...
I am task #19
```

```
I am task #20
I am task #21
sleeping...
I am task #22
sleeping...
I am task #23
I am task #24
sleeping...
sleeping...
```

As you can see, this is an easy way to set up a simple queuing service. It is not a lot of code, and you can get it running fairly quickly. In Part III, "Distributed Message Queues," we will go into further details on using distributed messaging queues.

MapReduce and Starfish

In theory, the concept of MapReduce is a simple one, and its name, sort of, indicates what it does. The MapReduce design paradigm is simple. It maps a collection of data and then reduces it to a smaller collection. The most famous implementation of MapReduce comes from Google. At Google MapReduce is known as the hammer. It is named that because it is the tool Google turns to most often to deal with its incredibly large sets of data.

Google's implementation of MapReduce is known to be incredibly complex, because it handles redundancy and failures and even detects slow machines. Google is known to run a million or more MapReduce programs a day. If that isn't an endorsement for why MapReduce is useful for processing large data sets, I don't know what is.

As I mentioned in the introduction to this chapter, Starfish ships with an implementation of the MapReduce paradigm. Starfish allows you to map either a collection of database objects, using the ActiveRecord[4] object relational mapping framework, or a flat file. Let's look at how Starfish approaches each of these types of datasets.

Alternative Implementations of MapReduce

Starfish isn't the only Ruby implementation of MapReduce available. It does happen to be the easiest to get up and running, however, which is why it is used to demonstrate MapReduce in this book.

SkyNet, http://skynet.rubyforge.org/, is an implementation
of MapReduce written by Adam Pisoni. It offers more features, customization, and tighter integration with Rails
than Starfish does. However, it does this at the expense of a
difficult setup and difficult-to-understand workflow. I have
heard good things about it, but I can't speak to it directly
because I had a tremendously difficult time getting it up
and running.

MRToolkit, http://code.google.com/p/mrtoolkit/, appeared
on the scene shortly after I had completed the first draft of
this book, so unfortunately I wasn't able to properly write
about it. The project came out, of all places, The New York
Times Company. The documentation suggests a fairly simple and well-thought-out API for creating MapReduce jobs.
MRToolkit sits atop the Apache Hadoop project,
http://hadoop.apache.org/, which it uses to do most of the
heavy lifting. Although installing and running Hadoop can
be a little cumbersome, it is a widely used and battle-tested
platform, which means that MRToolkit is definitely a
framework worth checking out.

Using Starfish to MapReduce ActiveRecord

To help demonstrate how to create MapReduce jobs with Starfish and ActiveRecord,
let's build an application that will process click logs we have stored in our database.
These logs get created when a user clicks a link on our site. We create an entry in the
database representing each click. We then need to do some processing on each of these
clicks. The problem we run into is that it can take up to 10 seconds to process each
click log, and it can be very CPU-intensive to do so. Because of that, we want to create a MapReduce that will distribute that workload across a lot of different computers.

Although getting Starfish to create a mapping of ActiveRecord objects is fairly
straightforward, we need to do a bit of prep work to get our examples set up so that
they'll run. Let's do that now so that we can get to the good stuff.

First, let's create our `ClickLog` model in a file called `click_log.rb`:

```
class ClickLog < ActiveRecord::Base

  def process
    logger.info("Processing #{self.url}...")
    time = Benchmark.realtime do
      sleep(rand(10))
      self.processed = true
      self.save!
    end
    logger.info("Processed #{self.url} in (#{time}) seconds.")
  end

end
```

Here we have a simple `ActiveRecord::Base` model, `ClickLog`. The model has a method called `process` that we need to call. It does the heavy lifting of processing our log entry, and it can take up to 10 seconds to run.

The `ClickLog` model needs a database table to speak to, so we must create a migration to generate that table. Of course, we don't have to create a migration. We could just create the table manually either through the command line or through a GUI tool of some sort, but this is a little easier. Let's create our migration in a folder called `migrations` and name it `20090730101359_create_starfish_db.rb`.[5] This migration should look like this:

```
class CreateStarfishDb < ActiveRecord::Migration

  def self.up
    create_table :click_logs do |t|
      t.string :url
      t.boolean :processed, :default => false
      t.timestamps
    end
  end

  def self.down
    drop_table :click_logs
  end

end
```

This creates a simple table called `click_logs` that has a column called `url` that houses the URL of the link the user clicked. It also has a column called `processed` that defaults to `false`. We will set it to `true` in the `process` method on the `Click-Log` model after we finish processing the record. This will prevent us from processing the record more than once.

Finally, we need a file that will establish a connection to a database for us, run the migration, if necessary, and populate some data for us. To do that, let's create a file called `ar_bootstrap.rb` and make it look like this:

```
require 'rubygems'
require 'active_record'
require 'benchmark'
require 'click_log'

logger = Logger.new(STDOUT)
logger.level = Logger::INFO
ActiveRecord::Base.logger = logger

ActiveRecord::Base.establish_connection({
  :database => 'starfish.db',
  :adapter => 'sqlite3'
})

ActiveRecord::Migrator.up('migrations')

if __FILE__ == $0
  100.times do |i|
    ClickLog.create!(:url => "/user/#{i+1}-#{Time.now.to_f}")
  end
end
```

This file looks more intimidating than it actually is. First we require certain necessary classes. In particular, we need to add the ActiveRecord libraries and our `Click-Log` model. After we do that, we need to configure ActiveRecord itself. ActiveRecord requires a logger, so we configure a fairly simple instance of `Logger` that logs `info` level or higher messages to `STDOUT` (standard out). We then assign that logger to `ActiveRecord::Base.logger`.

Next we need to establish a connection to our database. For our example, we will use the file-backed SQLite3[6] database. To configure this, we call the `establish_connection` method on `ActiveRecord::Base`. We tell it the name of the database, or, in our case, the filename we want to use, `starfish.db`, and which adapter we will be using, `sqlite3`.

After we have established a connection to our database (by the way, it creates the file for you so that you don't have to create it first), we can run the migration we created. We do that by calling the `up` method on `ActiveRecord::Migrator` and pointing it at the migrations directory we created earlier that has our migration in it.

Finally, at the bottom is some code that is designed to insert 100 records into the database. This code is found in the conditional statement at the bottom of the file; it looks like this:

```
if __FILE__ == $0
  100.times do |i|
    ClickLog.create!(:url => "/user/#{i+1}-#{Time.now.to_f}")
  end
end
```

This conditional block executes only if the current file that is being executed matches the name of our `ar_bootstrap.rb` file. This means that if we run the file directly, the conditional block executes. However, if we `require` the file, as we will be doing in another file, it does not execute the conditional block. The block simply loops 100 times and inserts 100 records into the `click_logs` table.

I admit that was a lot. But we're pretty much done with the setup. Before we get to the fun stuff, however, we need to run the `ar_bootstrap.rb` file so that we can create our database, our table, and populate it with some examples. We can do that like this:

```
$ ruby ar_bootstrap.rb
```

This should output the following:

```
Migrating to CreateStarfishDb (20090730101359)
== CreateStarfishDb: migrating
=================================================
-- create_table(:click_logs)
   -> 0.0874s
== CreateStarfishDb: migrated (0.0876s)
=====================================
```

Now that our database is created and we have some data to play with, let's create our server.

Earlier we talked about the different ways we can create a Starfish server—and client. I prefer not to use the "magic" trickery of the starfish binary and create a stand-alone executable file. This is my preference because it is very likely that you will create servers and clients that are executed from within another Ruby application, so by not tying our examples to the starfish binary we can easily port these scripts into larger libraries or applications without much trouble.

So, with that disclaimer out of the way, let's take a look at our server:

```ruby
ARGV.unshift('server.rb')

require 'rubygems'
require 'starfish'
require 'ar_bootstrap'

Starfish.server = lambda { |map_reduce|
  map_reduce.type = ClickLog
  map_reduce.conditions = ['processed = ?', false]
  map_reduce.queue_size = 10
  map_reduce.vigilant = true
}

Starfish.new('click_log_server').server
```

As mentioned earlier, we have to fool Starfish into thinking it's running from its binary. That is why we have to insert the server.rb filename into the ARGV system Array. Remember that we can "name" this server anything we want, not just server.rb. But that is what we have been using so far, so why break with tradition? We also need to require the Starfish libraries, as well as our ar_bootstrap file, so that we can have a connection to our database as well as access to our ClickLog model.

Inside our lambda we use to configure the server, we set four different configuration settings. First, we tell Starfish that the type, or class, we will serve up is ClickLog. Next, we tell it that we want to work on rows in the click_logs table only when the processed column is false. Third, we tell Starfish to fill the queue with only ten records from the database at a time. This is an important setting, because by default it pulls all the matching records from the database. This isn't good if that equals a million records!

These three parameters translate under the covers into the following ActiveRecord call:

```
ClickLog.find(:all,
              :conditions => ['processed = ?', false],
              :limit => 10)
```

The last setting, `vigilant`, tells Starfish whether it should exit the server when no more items are in the queue. By setting this value to `true`, we are telling Starfish to continue polling the database for new records forever, or until we stop the server manually. This is most likely the way you would want to run this type of example in real life, although it is nice to have the option for those one-off MapReduce jobs you want to run.

Finally, we start the server by naming it `click_log_server`.

Now our client code proves to be a lot simpler than the server code:

```
ARGV.unshift('client.rb')

require 'rubygems'
require 'starfish'
require 'ar_bootstrap'

Starfish.client = lambda do |click_log|
  click_log.process
end

Starfish.new('click_log_server').client
```

Again, we fool Starfish by making it think it is running from its binary and that the current file's name is `client.rb`. We require our necessary code, and then we create a `lambda` for Starfish to execute for each `ClickLog` record it receives from the server. In our `lambda` we simply call the `process` method that we defined in our `ClickLog` model.

With our client now in place, we can start everything and watch it work its magic. First we need to run the server. When the server starts, we should see the following printed to the screen:

```
server started for #<MapReduce:0x197c240
@time_spent_grabbing_objects=0.0, @offset=0,
@type=ClickLog(id: integer, url: string, processed: boolean,
created_at: datetime, updated_at: datetime),
@time_spent_grabbing_queues=0.0, @vigilant=true,
@input=["processed = ?", false], @num_objects_grabbed=0,
@lock=false, @queue=[], @num_queues_grabbed=0, @queue_size=10,
@time_began=0, @time_spent_processing_objects=0.0, @limit=1>
```

When we fire up our client, we should see that it starts to process the entries in our click_logs table:

```
Processing /user/1-1249009872.14215...
Processed /user/1-1249009872.14215 in (4.02453994750977) seconds.
Processing /user/2-1249009872.15377...
Processed /user/2-1249009872.15377 in (3.00500011444092) seconds.
Processing /user/3-1249009872.17103...
Processed /user/3-1249009872.17103 in (2.00500202178955) seconds.
Processing /user/4-1249009872.17533...
Processed /user/4-1249009872.17533 in (5.00495600700378) seconds.
```

I recommend that you start more instances of the client and see what happens. You'll see that the clients all start to get records to process. You'll also notice that none of the clients get the same record to process. That is because the server keeps track of who is processing what record. It makes sure not to hand out that record again, but rather to hand out the next record in the queue.

Using Starfish to MapReduce a File

ActiveRecord isn't the only input that Starfish can uses as a data source for your MapReduce programs. Starfish also reads through a file and delivers each line to each client, just like it did with each entry in the database when we were using Active-Record.

To start, let's create a simple file called file_bootstrap.rb that we can use to populate a file filled with click logs we want to process:

```ruby
File.open('clicks.log', 'w') do |f|
  100.times do |i|
    f.puts("/user/#{i+1}-#{Time.now.to_f}")
  end
end
```

This creates a new file called clicks.log and fills it with 100 URLs for us to process. Let's see what our server looks like for processing files compared to the server we used to dish out records in our database:

```
ARGV.unshift('server.rb')

require 'rubygems'
require 'starfish'

Starfish.server = lambda { |map_reduce|
  map_reduce.type = File
  map_reduce.input = "clicks.log"
  map_reduce.queue_size = 10
  map_reduce.lines_per_client = 5
  map_reduce.rescan_when_complete = false
}

Starfish.new('click_log_server').server
```

As you can see, we tell Starfish that the type of object we will serve up is a File. We then set the input to the clicks.log file we just created. As with our ActiveRecord implementation, we want to fill the queue with only ten entries at a time. In this case that means it will read the file ten lines at a time.

The next two configurations are unique to working with files. The first setting, lines_per_client, allows us to define how many lines of the file we want to send to the client at a time. Here we have set it to 5. This means that the client will be delivered an Array containing the five lines of the log file it has to process.

The last setting, rescan_when_complete, tells Starfish whether it should go back to the beginning of the file and start over. Although this might be useful on a few occasions, it is not helpful to us. In our example, if we had set this to true, it would just go back to the beginning of the file and start serving up each line again, causing us to forever be in a loop. To prevent an infinite loop, we will set it to false for now. As you will see in the following client, we are not removing the lines from the file, but rather just "processing" them.

Here's what our client looks like:

```
ARGV.unshift('client.rb')

require 'rubygems'
```

```ruby
require 'starfish'
require 'benchmark'

Starfish.client = lambda do |logs|
  logs.each do |click_log|
    click_log.strip!
    puts "Processing #{click_log}..."
    time = Benchmark.realtime do
      sleep(rand(10))
    end
    puts "Processed #{click_log} in (#{time}) seconds."
  end
end

Starfish.new('click_log_server').client
```

As you can see, we are given an `Array` containing lines from the file that needs to be processed. We loop through each of these lines and process them.

If we were to run both the server and the client, we would see the client success-fully processing the records it is given:

```
Processing /user/56-1249011703.70557...
Processed /user/56-1249011703.70557 in (3.00025391578674) seconds.
Processing /user/57-1249011703.70559...
Processed /user/57-1249011703.70559 in (5.00029587745667) seconds.
Processing /user/58-1249011703.7056...
Processed /user/58-1249011703.7056 in (3.00025296211243) seconds.
Processing /user/59-1249011703.70562...
Processed /user/59-1249011703.70562 in (4.00030207633972) seconds.
Processing /user/60-1249011703.70563...
Processed /user/60-1249011703.70563 in (2.00020003318787) seconds.
```

This is all there is to working with files and Starfish. As you can imagine, this can prove to be very useful when dealing with extremely large access or error logs that need processing.

Conclusion

In this chapter we put the Starfish library through its paces and looked at where it excels and where it falls down. Although Starfish didn't fare so well in our "Hello

World" and "Distributed Logger" applications, we saw that it really shined when we used it to build a distributed task processing system.

Starfish also proves its worth when you write MapReduce programs. Its simple integration with ActiveRecord and files makes it a snap to get up and running and start distributing the processing of these records across many different machines. On that note, though, it is a shame that Starfish doesn't have a way to write to an API for creating MapReduce tasks. It would be nice to be able to plug in another data source that isn't ActiveRecord or a file and not have to hand-roll it all.

Although this is definitely a well-written library, I found that it fails in a few areas. The areas in which Starfish doesn't succeed are easy to fix; I would love to see Lucas Carlson make a few changes. At that point I'm sure Starfish will be a more prominent player in the world of distributed programming with Ruby, particularly when it comes to writing MapReduce applications.

Carlson has built a very simple and easy-to-use library with Starfish that can make using distributed queues quite easy. A few bumps in the road occur with its use, but its ease of use should make the couple of simple hacks you need to do worth the hassle.

Endnotes

1. http://rufy.com/starfish/doc/

2. http://oreilly.com/catalog/9780596523695/

3. http://labs.google.com/papers/mapreduce.html, http://en.wikipedia.org/wiki/MapReduce

4. http://en.wikipedia.org/wiki/ActiveRecord_(Rails), http://ar.rubyonrails.org/. ActiveRecord can be installed using RubyGems: `$ gem install activerecord`

5. I know that seems like an awful name for any file. However, ActiveRecord has pretty strict requirements for the naming of its migrations. For example, each migration must start with a unique timestamp. The name that follows that has to be the underscored version of the migration class name. I know it's pretty crazy, but that's just the way it is.

6. http://www.sqlite.org/. In addition to having SQLite3 installed, you need to install the SQLite3 gem to have access from ActiveRecord to the SQLite3 libraries. This gem can be installed using RubyGems: `$ gem install sqlite3-ruby`.

Chapter 5
Distribunaut

In early 2008, I was working for a company that was using Ruby on Rails as the framework behind the application we were building. For the most part we were happy with Rails, but there were things we wanted to do that Rails was just not a good fit for. First we realized that what had started as a Web 2.0 application was anything but that. Instead, we came to the conclusion that we were building a rather large portal application.

For all of its pros, Rails has a few cons as well. I won't go into all of them now, but the biggest disadvantage we found was that Rails doesn't want to help you write complex portal applications. It wants you to build smaller, simpler applications—at least, at the time it did. With Rails 3.0 on the horizon, that may change.

In addition to building this large portal, we decided we wanted to split our application into many applications. The advantages we saw were smaller code bases that were easier to maintain and separate applications that were easier to scale. We also could push updates and new features sooner, because we didn't have a gigantic code base to worry about.

We identified three main problems. First, we wanted to let each application maintain its own set of routing, but we wanted the other applications to be able to use the dynamic routing we had become accustomed to in Rails. We didn't want to hardcode URLs in the other applications; we wanted them generated by the application they would be linking to. Second, we wanted to share views and layouts among these applications. We didn't want to have to deal with SVN externals, GIT submodules, or symlinks. We wanted to be able to quickly say, "Here is a URL for a layout. Render it like you would a local layout." Finally, we wanted to share models and libraries through-out all these applications without having to worry about packaging them and rede-ploying all these applications each time we made a bug fix to a model.

With these goals in mind, I set out to find a Ruby web framework that would help us achieve these goals. After downloading and testing nearly 20 frameworks, I was at a loss for the solution we needed. Then I found Rack.[1] Rack bills itself as a framework for frameworks. It is a middleware abstraction layer that lets framework developers get on with developing their framework without worrying about things like parsing requests and talking with application servers. Within a few hours I had a simple MVC-based framework up and running, and the Mack Framework was born.

I then spent the next year building and developing a large feature set for Mack, including all the libraries to handle distributed routes, views, and models. During that time I was asked time and again to make these components available outside the Mack framework for others to use. In April 2009, I announced an early version of a library I dubbed Distribunaut.

Distribunaut[2] is a port of one-third of the distributed features that are found in Mack. In particular, it focuses on making it incredibly easy to distribute models and other Ruby classes. You will not find distributed views/layouts and routes in Distri-bunaut. The reason is that they are too specific to each of the web frameworks out there, and coding for each one would be a lot of work.

So with that brief history of Distribunaut, let's look at what it can do for us.

Installation

Installing the Distribunaut library is simple. It can be installed using RubyGems:

```
$ gem install markbates-distribunaut -s http://gems.github.com
```

You should then see something similar to the following, telling you that you have suc-cessfully installed the gem:

```
Successfully installed markbates-distribunaut-0.2.1
```

Blastoff: Hello, World!

Distribunaut uses DRb and Rinda to do most of its heavy lifting. The good news is that because you have already learned all about DRb and Rinda, you can easily jump into experimenting with Distribunaut.

As you'll remember from our look at Rinda, we need to start a RingServer before we can run any code. Distribunaut ships with a convenient binary to help make starting, stopping, and restarting a RingServer easy:

```
$ distribunaut_ring_server start
```

If you wanted to stop the RingServer, you would do so with the following command:

```
$ distribunaut_ring_server stop
```

You can probably guess how to restart the server. You should restart the RingServer between all these examples, just so things don't go a bit funny on you:

```
$ distribunaut_ring_server restart
```

So, with a RingServer running nicely as a daemon in the background, let's kick off things with a simple "Hello World" application. Let's start with a server. Keep in mind that, as we talked about earlier in the book, when we are using DRb and Rinda, applications can act as both a server and a client. So when we use the term "server" here, we are merely using it to describe a bit of code that serves up some content. So what does our HelloWorld class look like with Distribunaut? Let's see:

```ruby
require 'rubygems'
require 'distribunaut'

configatron.distribunaut.app_name = :hello_world_app

class HelloWorld
  include Distribunaut::Distributable
```

```
def say_hi
  "Hello, World!"
end

end

DRb.thread.join
```

First we require `rubygems` and then the `Distribunaut` library itself. After that we hit the first of two lines that make Distribunaut special.

Each Distribunaut "application" needs a unique name. When we talk about applications within Distribunaut, we are actually talking about a Ruby VM/process that contains one or more Distribunaut classes. The name of that application should be unique to avoid confusion. We will look at what can happen with redundant application, and class, names a bit later in this chapter.

To manage its configurations, Distribunaut uses the Configatron[3] library. We set the application as follows:

```
configatron.distribunaut.app_name = :hello_world_app
```

This needs to happen only once per Ruby VM. If you set it multiple times, strange things can happen, so be careful. In our sample code we are setting the application name to `:hello_world_app`. We could just as easily set it to something like `:server1` if we wanted to make it more generic for other Distribunaut classes we were planning on running in the same Ruby VM.

After we have set up our application name, the only other thing we have to do is include the `Distribunaut::Distributable` module in our `HelloWorld` class. Then we are ready to try to get a "Hello, World!" remotely.

Before we get to our client code, let's take a quick look at what the preceding `HelloWorld` class would've looked like had we used raw `DRb` and `Rinda`:

```
require 'rinda/ring'

class HelloWorld
  include DRbUndumped

  def say_hi
    "Hello, World!"
  end
```

```
  end

  DRb.start_service
  ring_server = Rinda::RingFinger.primary
  ring_server.write([:hello_world_service, :HelloWorld,
                  HelloWorld.new, 'I like to say hi!'],
                Rinda::SimpleRenewer.new)

  DRb.thread.join
```

Although the `HelloWorld` class part of it is relatively the same, much more noise is required at the end to get our `HelloWorld` instance into the `RingServer`. At this point it is also worth pointing out that in the `Rinda` version of `HelloWorld` we had to create a new instance of the class. This means that we can't call any class methods that `HelloWorld` may have. This includes the ability to call the `new` method and get a new instance of the `HelloWorld` class. We are stuck with that instance only. We did not do anything of the sort with the Distribunaut version of the class. In fact, you probably have noticed that we didn't make any calls to get it into the `RingServer`. We'll talk about why that is shortly. First, let's look at our client code:

```
  require 'rubygems'
  require 'distribunaut'

  hw = Distribunaut::Distributed::HelloWorld.new
  puts hw.say_hi
```

If we were to run this code, we should see the following output:

```
  Hello, World!
```

What just happened there? Where did the `Distribunaut::Distributed::HelloWorld` class come from? How did it know to print "Hello, World!" when we called the `say_hi` method? All great questions.

The `Distribunaut::Distributed` module is "special." When you preface a constant such as `HelloWorld` in that module, it queries the `RingServer` and attempts to find a service that matches that constant. So, in our case it searched the `RingServer` for a service called `HelloWorld`. It found the `HelloWorld` class we created earlier and returned a reference to it. With that reference we could call the `new`

method on that class, which returned a new instance of the `HelloWorld` class. And
then we could call the `say_hi` method.

So if we didn't explicitly place our `HelloWorld` class in the `RingServer`, how did
we access it? And how were we able to call a class method on it, when we know that
you have to put instances only into a `RingServer`? The same answer applies to both
questions. When we included the `Distribunaut::Distributable` module into the
`HelloWorld` class, it created a Singleton wrapper class on-the-fly that then proxies all
methods called on that proxy class onto the original `HelloWorld` class. With that we
can put the Singleton instance into the `RingServer`. Then we can call class methods,
which allows us to do things like call the `new` and get back a new instance of the class.

Having all of this happen automatically also helps clean up the usual supporting
code you need to write to both set an instance into the `RingServer` and retrieve that
instance later. Just look at what a plain-vanilla `DRb` and `Rinda` implementation of the
client would look like:

```
require 'rinda/ring'

DRb.start_service
ring_server = Rinda::RingFinger.primary

service = ring_server.read([:hello_world_service,
                            nil, nil, nil])
server = service[2]

puts server.say_hi
```

This is not only more code, but also uglier code.

Building a Distributed Logger with Distribunaut

So now that you have a good understanding of how Distribunaut works, and what it
does under the covers, let's try to create a distributed logger and see how it goes. To
create our distributed logger, we want to create a `RemoteLogger` class. Here's what
that would look like:

```
require 'rubygems'
require 'distribunaut'
require 'logger'
```

```
configatron.distribunaut.app_name = :remote_logger

LOGGER = ::Logger.new(STDOUT)

class RemoteLogger
  include Distribunaut::Distributable

  class << self

    def new
      LOGGER
    end

    [:debug, :info, :warn, :error, :fatal].each do |meth|
      define_method(meth) do |*args|
        LOGGER.send(meth, *args)
      end
    end

  end

end

DRb.thread.join
```

Although this looks a lot more intimidating than our HelloWorld class, it really isn't. The extra code comes from making it a bit easier to access the underlying Ruby Logger class we want to wrap. We could have just harnessed the incredible power of Ruby and opened up the Logger class and included the Distribunaut::Distributable module directly into it, but that is generally not considered good practice. Besides, this way lets us talk about a few things we couldn't talk about otherwise. Let's look at it in a bit more depth; you'll see it isn't that complex.

After we require the correct classes and define our application name (this time we are calling it :remote_logger), we create a constant called LOGGER to act as a holder for our Logger instance. We want only one instance of the Logger class. That is why we assign it to the global constant—so that we can access it throughout the rest of our code.

After we have included the Distribunaut::Distributable module into our RemoteLogger class, we then add a few methods for convenience. The first of these methods is a class-level override of the new method. We do this so that when our

clients try to create a new instance of the RemoteLogger class, they are actually getting the wrapped Logger class instead. Next we generate the five standard logging
methods on Logger, putting them at the class level of the RemoteLogger class. These
methods simply proxy the methods onto the single instance of our Logger class that
we have stored in our LOGGER constant. We do this so that our clients can call these
methods at the class level of RemoteLogger without having to create a new instance
of it. This is easier to demonstrate in the client code.

With all of that out of the way, let's see what our client code would look like:

```
require 'rubygems'
require 'distribunaut'

logger = Distribunaut::Distributed::RemoteLogger.new

logger.debug("Hello, World!")

Distribunaut::Distributed::RemoteLogger.error("oops!")
```

In this client we first create a new "instance" of the RemoteLogger class. I put
"instance" in quotes for a reason. Remember that we don't actually get a new instance
of the RemoteLogger class. Instead, we simply get back a reference to the global
instance of the Logger class we set up earlier.

As soon as we have the RemoteLogger, we can call the standard logging methods, such as debug. We should see our message printed to the server's screen, not the
client's. After we call the debug method, we call the class method error on the
RemoteLogger class and pass it the message "oops!".

If we were to run all of this, we would get the following:

```
Hello, World!
oops!
```

As you can see, creating a new distributed logger with Distribunaut is actually
quite easy. We could have simplified the code by not giving class-level convenience
methods for the common logging methods. But it was only a few more lines of code,
and it could make the end user's life a little easier.

Avoiding Confusion of Services

Earlier, when speaking about application names, I mentioned that names need to be unique to avoid confusion, but I didn't explain what I meant.

You know from Chapter 2, "Rinda," that when we create a `Tuple` to put into the `RingServer`, we give it some unique characteristics that allow us to retrieve it easily. The combination of these characteristics becomes sort of like an ID for that particular `Tuple`. So imagine if we were to put two `Tuples` into the `RingServer` that had the same characteristics. How would we retrieve the specific one we want? If we use the same application name, we not only run the risk of overwriting another `Tuple`, but we also make it difficult to find later.

As you have seen, Distribunaut performs a lot of magic that keeps us from having to write as much code. It also makes the code we write cleaner and easier to use and maintain. One thing Distribunaut does for you is build the search characteristics for you when you make a call to the special `Distribunaut::Distributed` module. When Distribunaut goes to build the search parameters for that request, it takes into account only the class, or service, name you provide. Because of this, if you have two applications serving up a class with the same name, you are unsure which one you will receive from the query. In some cases this might be fine, but in other cases, it might be a problem.

Let's look at a simple example. Let's create a service that serves up a `User` class. We want to launch at least two instances of this service for this example. To do that we need to run the following code twice to start two instances of it:

```
require 'rubygems'
require 'distribunaut'

user_servers = ['0']

services = Distribunaut::Utils::Rinda.available_services

services.each do |service|
  if service.app_name.to_s.match(/^user_server_(\d+)$/)
    user_servers << "#{$1}"
  end
end
```

```
user_servers.sort!

app_name = "user_server_#{user_servers.last.succ}"

puts "Launching: #{app_name}"

configatron.distribunaut.app_name = app_name

class User
  include Distribunaut::Distributable

  def app_server_name
    configatron.distribunaut.app_name
  end

end

DRb.thread.join
```

A large majority of the preceding code simply finds out what the last service, if there is one, was called. Then it names the service that is currently launching so that it has a unique name. Although most of this is straightforward Ruby code, it is worth pointing out the call to the `available_services` method on the `Distribunaut::Utils::Rinda` module. The `available_services` method, as its name implies, returns an `Array` of the services that are currently registered with Distribunaut. The elements of this `Array` are `Distribunaut::Tuple` classes, which are simply a convenience class to make it easier to deal with `Tuples` that are in the Distribunaut format.

After we have decided on an appropriate application name and registered it, we create a `User` class, include the `Distribunaut::Distributable` module and give it an instance method that returns the application name that is running this service.

Now, with a couple of instances of our service running, let's look at the style of client we have been using so far in this chapter:

```
require 'rubygems'
require 'distribunaut'

user = Distribunaut::Distributed::User.new
puts user.app_server_name
```

So which instance of the user service do we get when we run this? Well, on my system I see the following printed:

```
user_server_1
```

On your system you might see this:

```
user_server_2
```

or another variation, depending on how many instances you have running. There is no guarantee which instance you will receive when accessing services this way. Again, this might be acceptable in your environment, or it might not.

So what do you do when this is unacceptable, or you want to get a specific instance of a service? Distribunaut provides you with a method called `lookup`. This method is found on the `Distribunaut::Distributed` module. The `lookup` method takes a URL to find the specific instance you are looking for.

Right about now you should be wondering how you are supposed to know the URL of the service you want to look up. Don't worry. Distribunaut has you covered by making it easy to look up these services. Let's look at a client that wants to find specific instances of the user services we have running:

```
require 'rubygems'
require 'distribunaut'

user_one_url = "distributed://user_server_1/User"
UserOne = Distribunaut::Distributed.lookup(user_one_url)

user_two_url = "distributed://user_server_2/User"
UserTwo = Distribunaut::Distributed.lookup(user_two_url)

user1 = UserOne.new
puts user1.app_server_name

user2 = UserTwo.new
puts user2.app_server_name
```

Building the URL for the service we want is quite simple. The format is `distributed://<application_name>/<service_name>`. Because of this format, it is important that we have unique application names for each Ruby VM so that we can easily seek out the one we are looking for.

With the URLs in hand for the two services we are looking for, we can call the `lookup` method and find these two services. When we have them, we can create new instances of the `User` class and print the return value of the `app_server_name` method. You should see something similar to the following printed:

```
user_server_1
user_server_2
```

With the `lookup` method now in our arsenal, we can code with confidence, knowing that we will always get the specific instance of a service we are looking for. And we can do it without having to deal with IP addresses, ports, and other such nonsense.

Borrowing a Service with Distribunaut

As you probably remember from Chapter 2, when we retrieve `Tuples` from the `RingServer`, we have two choices. We can either read the `Tuple` or take the `Tuple`. The former leaves the `Tuple` in the `RingServer` for others to access simultaneously. The latter removes the `Tuple` from the `RingServer`; as a consequence, no one else can gain access to that `Tuple`.

So what happens when we access a service using Distribunaut? Are we doing a read or a take from the `RingServer`? Distribunaut does a read from the `RingServer`, thereby allowing others to access the same service at the same time.

Most of the time this is the exact behavior you want. You usually want to be a good citizen and let others access the service you are accessing as well. Sometimes, however, you might need to grab hold of a service exclusively, do a few things with that service, and then return it to the `RingServer` for others to have access to.

So how do we take a service from the `RingServer`, use that service, and then return it for wider use? We could use raw `Rinda` and `DRb` code, but that would be ugly, and prone to error should any of the underpinnings of Distribunaut change. Instead, Distribunaut offers the concept of borrowing a service.

To demonstrate how to borrow a service, let's use our simple `HelloWorld` class as the service we want to borrow:

```
require 'rubygems'
require 'distribunaut'

configatron.distribunaut.app_name = :hello_world_app

class HelloWorld
  include Distribunaut::Distributable

  def say_hi
    "Hello, World!"
  end

end

DRb.thread.join
```

Here is what our client code would look like to borrow the `HelloWorld` service:

```
require 'rubygems'
require 'distribunaut'

Distribunaut::Distributed::HelloWorld.borrow do |hw_class|
  hw = hw_class.new
  puts hw.say_hi
  begin
    hw = Distribunaut::Distributed::HelloWorld.new
  rescue Rinda::RequestExpiredError => e
    puts "Oops - We couldn't find the HelloWorld class!"
  end

end

hw = Distribunaut::Distributed::HelloWorld.new
puts hw.say_hi
```

If we were to run this code, we should see the following printed:

```
Hello, World!
Oops - We couldn't find the HelloWorld class!
Hello, World!
```

So exactly what did we do, and how did it work? The `borrow` method takes a block and yields a reference to our proxy service, as we discussed earlier in this chapter. This works the same way as if we had called `Distribunaut::Distributed::HelloWorld` directly. The difference is, before the block gets executed, the service is located and removed from the `RingServer`. It is then "locked" and placed back into the `RingServer` in such a way that others can't retrieve it. After the block finishes executing, the service is unlocked in the `RingServer` and is available again for public consumption.

If we look at what is happening in the block, we see that we call the `new` method on the `hw_class` variable, which is the reference to the `HelloWorld` service. The `new` method creates a new instance of the `HelloWorld` class, and we can call the `say_hi` method on it.

To demonstrate that we can't access the `HelloWorld` service directly, we attempt to call it, but, as we see, it raises a `Rinda::RequestExpiredError` because the service cannot be found.

After the block has finished executing, we again try to access the `HelloWorld` service as we would normally. This time, instead of an exception, we are greeted with a pleasant "Hello, World!".

As you can see, the concept of borrowing a service allows us to easily take control of the service we want, do the work we need to do on that service, and then have it automatically returned to the `RingServer` for others to use. It also has the added benefit of being quite easy to code. We don't have to write fragile code that takes the service from the `RingServer`, handles exceptions that may arise, and ensures that the service gets placed back into the `RingServer` correctly.

Conclusion

Obviously I'm slightly biased in my feelings about Distribunaut, seeing as how I am the developer of the library. With that said, I feel strongly that Distribunaut makes distributed objects incredibly easy to code, use, and maintain.

The library continues to grow and develop. Its fundamentals were pulled from the mack-distributed gem for the Mack Framework, but the library has grown and evolved much since its origins. Even during the course of writing this chapter, I found several bugs, enhancements, and performance improvements that could be made, so I made changes. The underpinnings of this library have been working hard in several production environments and have proven themselves to be reliable, fast, and easy to use.

Overall I feel that the simple interface, basically just including a module, makes an already easy system for building distributed applications, DRb and Rinda, even easier. Instead of having to write code to look up services, read them, parse them, manage them, and so on, you can use something you are already familiar with—simple Ruby objects.

What does the future hold for Distribunaut? As far as the feature set is concerned, that is hard to say. I try to develop features that will actually be used, not features that I think are cool. What I can tell you for sure is that Distribunaut will continue to be maintained and grown to keep up with the challenges of developing distributed applications.

Endnotes

1. http://rack.rubyforge.org/

2. http://github.com/markbates/distribunaut/tree/master

3. http://github.com/markbates/configatron/tree/master

CHAPTER 6

Politics

In November of 2008, I presented "Building Distributed Applications" at RubyConf. The day after my presentation, I saw a gentleman by the name of Mike Perham[1] present a project he was working on, called "Politics." I remember thinking that it seemed like an interesting idea, but I didn't quite get what he was trying to do at the time. I squirreled it away as something to keep my eye on and eventually try to figure out.

Fast-forward several months, and I'm at work discussing with a colleague a problem we are having. We have identical application server instances running in production, using a popular "cloud" hosting provider. Each one of these instances is born of the same base image, meaning that each instance is loaded with the same software and is configured identically. With autoscaling, the automated launching of a new instance in response to load, we are not always in charge of launching an instance; the "cloud" does it for us.

The problem we were running into was this: How do we configure just one machine to run our background jobs, scheduled tasks, and other queue-type processing? We didn't want each machine to perform these tasks for a couple reasons. First, we didn't want to worry about each of these processes to step on the other's toes, processing the same task. Second, we didn't want to add load to each instance, when we could burden just one instance.

The problem came to be, how do we do this? How do we configure one instance to perform these tasks, and not the others, when they are all identical instances? Also, what if the instance we configure crashes or goes down? Do we then have to manually configure another instance to be the one that performs the tasks?

We chewed on these questions over lunch, and we couldn't come up with a decent solution that made us both happy. A few days later I was watching a popular Sunday morning political roundtable talk show, and I remembered Perham's Politics.[2] I sat down, started to play with the software, and realized two things: It might solve our problems, and it was easy to use.

Politics provides modules that allow us to build a self-repairing worker class that can be run on all our instances. But it designates only one instance at a time to do the work specified for a given time period. Politics calls this worker a token worker.

Under the covers Politics uses three different technologies to maintain order in all the worker classes. One of them we already know—DRb. The other two technologies it uses are Memcached[3] and mDNS[4] (also known as Multicast DNS, Zero Configuration Networking, or Bonjour).[5]

Memcached

Over the past few years, Memcached has become an industry-standard mechanism used to cache—well, pretty much everything. It is nearly impossible to be a developer and not hear the word Memcached mentioned as a must-have technology.

Originally designed to cache database queries, Memcached is now used to cache everything from HTML to whole objects. Its easy setup and straightforward clients, written in nearly every modern language, have helped ensure its continued success.

Memcached, at its most basic, is a high-performance `Hash`. Written in C, Memcached allows the setting and retrieval of key/value pairs, along with basic expiration data. Memcached automatically expires objects at their set expiration time. If an expiration time is not set, it retains that object for the life of the Memcached instance. The only exception to this rule is that Memcached has very smart algorithms for clearing out old, unused data, should it need to make space for more often-used objects.

In an effort to keep Memcached as lean and mean as it can be, the developers have kept its feature set incredibly light. For example, you can't even get a list of all the keys currently stored within Memcached. Although the lack of a large feature set is a negative for some, that same lack of features allows for a highly stable and high-performance code base.

mDNS: a Horse of Many Colors

Although it may have many names, mDNS, or whatever your preferred name for it is, was developed to allow developers to use familiar DNS interfaces and techniques when in a small network where no DNS server has been installed. This technology is commonly encountered when trying to set up a network printer or storage device.

As briefly mentioned earlier in this book, `Rinda` uses this technology to find available services on the local network. Politics uses mDNS for the same reason one would use `Rinda`—to discover available services. It is unclear to me why the author of Politics, Mike Perham, decided to use mDNS and not `Rinda` for the discovery portion of Politics.

Installation

To use Politics, you must first have both Memcached and mDNS installed on your system. If you are using Mac OS X, you already have mDNS installed. The same goes for most flavors of UNIX. If your system does not have mDNS installed already, consult the package management system for your operating system to find out how to install it. Memcached will need to be installed on most machines. Instructions on how to do this can be found at http://www.danga.com/memcached/.

After you have installed, or confirmed the installation of, Memcached and mDNS, you can easily install Politics using RubyGems:

```
$ gem install mperham-politics -s http://gems.github.com
```

You should see a message similar to the following:

```
Successfully installed mperham-politics-0.2.5
```

With that, your installation should be complete, and you should be ready to go.

Where's "Hello World"?

This is the only chapter that doesn't start with a simple "Hello World" example. Throughout this book I have tried to keep the format of the beginning of each chapter the same. This gives each library and tool a common point for evaluation. Plus, it helps ensure that everything is installed and working correctly.

I struggled quite a lot with Politics to try and find a way to make it fit this model I had in mind for each chapter. The problem, it turns out, is that Politics is very different from each of the other libraries and tools we look at in this book.

It is not a tool that allows effective communication between different services, so it is not easy to just set up a simple "Hello World" example. Instead, Politics, as you will see, is a set of utilities that lets you solve problems involved with using some of the other tools in this book, such as making sure that different processes work in harmony.

Because of how different Politics is from the other libraries discussed in this book, I decided to treat it as such. I wanted you, the reader, to see Politics for what it is and show you how it can be leveraged with other technologies in this book to further enhance your distributed applications.

Working with Politics

As I mentioned earlier, one of the problems I was having was making sure that all the processes I had running didn't step on each others' toes and spend cycles doing the same work. This is a common problem when dealing with distributed programming. A typical example occurs when we are working with distributed message queues. Part III of this book, "Distributed Message Queues," discusses distributed messaging queues in greater detail. For now, simply know that what we discuss in this section can make processing those queues extremely effective and powerful.

For our example, let's pretend we have just received a big juicy government contract. The government has a queue that is constantly being filled with how much pork-barrel spending is happening. Because so much spending is occurring, the government wants to ensure that the system is constantly running and self-repairing. Should any of the workers die, or be taken offline, another should take its place and continue to keep track of the pork that is being spent.

To help us solve this problem, Politics offers the `Politics::TokenWorker` module. What does this module offer us? The `Politics::TokenWorker` module, when included into a worker class, allows us to create a class that will either process the work we give it and act as the "leader," or patiently sit and wait for its turn to be the "leader" while not doing any work. The beautiful part of what the `Politics::TokenWorker` module offers is that no extra coding is needed to figure out if the current instance of the class is a "worker" or a "leader."

Right now you are probably wondering what the difference is between a leader and a worker. When we launch our classes that include the `Politics::TokenWorker` module, they are all the same—they are workers. Workers, in this case, are the opposite of what you might believe them to be. Workers actually don't do any work. Instead, workers sit and wait for their chance to be a leader. Leaders, on the other hand, do all the work. I know—it seems a bit confusing, doesn't it? I probably would have chosen slightly different names, but that's just me.

When a worker or workers launch, they all connect to the instance of Memcached that they are configured to communicate with. When they do that, one of the instances gets a token (hence the name token worker) and becomes a leader for a specified interval. It is then the job of that leader to complete the tasks assigned during the given time period, or iteration length, as it is known in Politics. When the specified time frame has elapsed, all the instances again connect to Memcached, where one of them is again elected leader, and the cycle continues.

Let's look at an example of how this works in practice. To start, we need a queue to serve all the pork that needs to be processed. The following class is that queue:

```ruby
require 'fileutils'

class PorkSpendingQueue

  def self.pop
    queue = Dir.glob(File.join(pork_spending_dir, '*.pork'))
    queue.sort! {|x, y| y <=> x}
    pork = queue.pop
    if pork
      val = File.read(pork)
      FileUtils.rm(pork)
      return val
    end
    return nil
  end

  def self.start_spending
    FileUtils.mkdir_p(pork_spending_dir)
    100.times do
      f_name = (rand(99999999) * rand(99999999)).to_s[0..10]
      pork_file = File.join(pork_spending_dir,
                            "#{f_name}.pork")
      File.open(pork_file, 'w') do |f|
        f.write("$#{f_name}")
      end
    end
  end

  def self.pork_spending_dir
    File.join(File.dirname(__FILE__), 'pork_spending')
  end

end

if __FILE__ == $0
  PorkSpendingQueue.start_spending
end
```

Although the `PorkSpendingQueue` should not be used in production, I highly recommend one of the great queues discussed in Part III of this book. It should certainly serve our simple needs. The `pop` method finds the smallest piece of pork that is stored on the file system, reads the contents of the file, deletes that file, and returns the file's value. Should we run out of pork (which is highly unlikely), `nil` will be returned.

The `start_spending` method quite generously creates a bunch of pork for us in our queue. To make sure you have pork for the following examples, you should execute the `start_spending` method to fill your queue.

Now that we have a queue we can access, let's see what our token worker class will look like:

```ruby
require 'rubygems'
require 'politics'
require 'politics/token_worker'
require 'pork_spending_queue'

class PorkSpendingTokenWorker
  include Politics::TokenWorker

  def initialize
    register_worker('pork_spending_token_worker',
                    :iteration_length => 10,
                    :servers => memcached_servers)
  end

  def start
    process do
      5.times do
        pork = PorkSpendingQueue.pop
        if pork
          puts "PID (#{$$}) just spent: #{pork}"
        end
        sleep 1
      end
    end
  end
end
```

```
def memcached_servers
  ['127.0.0.1:11211']
end

end

p = PorkSpendingTokenWorker.new
p.start
```

First we need to require a couple of Politics' files, `politics` and `politics/`
`token_worker`. When we have those, we require our `pork_spending_queue` file so
that we can access our `PorkSpendingQueue` class that we built earlier.

In the definition of our `PorkSpendingTokenWorker`, we include the
`Politics::TokenWorker` module to give us access to the methods and hooks we
need to make our class into a token worker.

In our `initialize` method we need to connect this class to the system. We do
that by calling the `register_worker` method we got when we included the
`Politics::TokenWorker` module. The `register_worker` method takes two
parameters. The first is the name of the group this worker should belong to. The second parameter is a `Hash` of options. Currently, only two options are supported.

The first is `:iteration_length`. This option is how long, in seconds, you want
an iteration to be. An iteration is the span of time between when a leader is elected
and when another leader needs to be elected. It is important to pick the correct length
of time for your iteration. You want to make sure that it is long enough to actually
process the tasks given to it. If you set this parameter too short, an exception is raised
and the instance of that worker dies, never to be heard from again. However, if you
set this parameter too long, there are other issues to deal with. First, if you set your
worker up to process only so many tasks in the iteration length, then it will just sit
there doing nothing after it finishes processing the tasks while it waits for the iteration
to end. Second, if there is a problem with the current leader, a new one won't be
elected until the next iteration. So if you set your length to be an hour and your leader
dies five minutes in, then you will have to wait another 55 minutes for the next leader
to be elected. Although this might work for you in some circumstances, it is probably
not going to work for you in most situations. The moral of this story is to take some
time, do some benchmarking, and try to determine the most appropriate time for
your system.

The second parameter is `:servers`. This parameter is an `Array` of Memcached
server locations, presented in the format *host:port*.

With our `PorkSpendingTokenWorker` registered with the system, we need to tell it what it should do if it becomes a leader. We define this within our `start` method. There is no requirement that this method name needs to be called `start`. In theory, you do not even need a particular method; you could put it in your `initialize` method. But I prefer to have my code a bit cleaner than that—hence the separate method.

In our `start` method, we call the `process` method provided by the `Politics::TokenWorker` module. The `process` method is provided a block that tells the leader what to work on when the time comes. In our block we tell the class to process five pieces of pork per iteration. We call the `pop` method on the `PorkSpendingQueue` class. If a piece of pork is returned to us (not a `nil` value), we print a message to the screen. It tells us which `PID`, or process, has just spent the pork, and how much pork has been spent. After we have processed a piece of pork, we sleep for 1 second.

At the bottom of our file you will notice these two lines:

```
p = PorkSpendingTokenWorker.new
p.start
```

These lines are there so that if you execute the file, it will create a new instance of the `PorkSpendingTokenWorker` class and call its `start` method.

Now if we execute this class, we should see something similar to the following get printed to our screen:

```
I, [2009-06-20T23:31:23.335687 #2147]  INFO -- :
macbates.home:2147 elected leader at Sat Jun 20 23:31:23 -0400 2009
PID (2147) just spent: $14189445159
PID (2147) just spent: $14212980111
PID (2147) just spent: $14214658458
PID (2147) just spent: $14231583625
PID (2147) just spent: $14298736695
I, [2009-06-20T23:31:33.336948 #2147]  INFO -- : macbates.home:2147
elected leader at Sat Jun 20 23:31:33 -0400 2009
PID (2147) just spent: $14363023820
PID (2147) just spent: $14382726209
PID (2147) just spent: $14545065772
```

Now if you were to start a second instance of the `PorkSpendingTokenWorker` class, you would see that it will, most likely, just sit there idle. There is a possibility that at the end of the iteration it might become a leader, but I have found that in most cases the original stays the leader until it is killed. This is not always the case, however, and you certainly should not count on it when developing these classes.

Caveats

The documentation that ships with Politics points out a few caveats that also should be mentioned here.

The first caveat is that Politics is not designed to work with multiple processes within the same Ruby VM. This means that we cannot fire up two instances of the `PorkSpendingTokenWorker` class in the same Ruby VM. If you want more than one instance of the class working on the same machine or virtual instance, you need to create a new Ruby VM for each instance.

The reason given for not being able to run more than one instance of a Politics class is that the algorithm used to choose a leader is only designed to pick a leader from a set of processes, not multiple instances within a single process.

The second caveat was briefly touched on in the main text. The algorithm that selects the next leader is not guaranteed to choose the previous leader for the next iteration. It has been my experience that most of the time, when a leader is elected, it tends to remain the leader for a long time; however, this is not certain.

You should not architect your classes to assume that there is a guaranteed order to the selection of a leader. Classes should be designed with the idea that they will be a leader only once. This means that you should avoid keeping state information pertinent to the leader in a particular Ruby VM. If you need to store such information, you should place it in a database, Memcached, or other such storage that can be accessed by any instance that is chosen to be the leader.

If we were to kill the instance that is currently the leader, we should see that the other, still running instance should become elected leader at the end of the current iteration:

```
I, [2009-06-20T23:31:45.417060 #2177]  INFO -- :
macbates.home:2177 elected leader at Sat Jun 20 23:31:45 -0400 2009
PID (2177) just spent: $14889841421
PID (2177) just spent: $14922721224
PID (2177) just spent: $14998700813
PID (2177) just spent: $15017841045
PID (2177) just spent: $15033730512
```

As you can see, a different process took over as leader and continued to work on processing our pork queue.

Conclusion

Earlier in the chapter I described a problem I was having. I had identical server instances, but I wanted only one to work on background tasks at a time. I also needed to make sure that if a new instance was brought online, either by me or automatically by the system, it didn't start processing background tasks. I also had the rather common problem of making sure that if the instance that was doing the background tasks died, another instance would pick up the mantle and start processing the background tasks.

Politics managed to solve those problems for me. By writing a simple class I was able to start instances of that class on each server instance when it starts, and I could rest assured that only one instance of the class would be processing tasks at any given time. I also could take comfort in the knowledge that should one of my instances die, or need to be taken offline for any reason, another instance would kick in to do the processing.

There certainly are other ways to solve this problem. A technology such as Delayed Job (Chapter 10, "Delayed Jobs") also could be used, but it takes a different approach to solving these problems. I will say that eventually I did stop using Politics in favor of Delayed Job. That was not a slight on Politics but rather a desire to have a unified system for dealing with processing tasks. You might be wondering why I still chose to write about Politics, despite having stopped using it myself. The reason is that it is a good demonstration of using token workers for managing distributed programming tasks, plus there definitely are places where it is a more appropriate technology than something else like Delayed Job.

The library has a few shortcomings; the biggest one for me is the use of mDNS and not `Rinda` for its autodiscovery backend. However, it is well written, and it definitely gets the job done. Later in the book, when we look at tools such as distributed message queues, I want you to keep Politics in mind. Think about how using Politics will allow you to keep on top of your queues in an easy-to-use, easy-to-configure fashion.

Endnotes

1. http://www.mikeperham.com/

2. http://github.com/mperham/politics/tree/master

3. http://www.danga.com/memcached/

4. http://en.wikipedia.org/wiki/MDNS, http://www.multicastdns.org/

5. http://en.wikipedia.org/wiki/Bonjour_(software)

PART III
Distributed
Message Queues

Part I of this book looked what the standard Ruby library offers for free right out of the box. Part II took that knowledge and leveraged it to examine a handful of tools and frameworks designed to take what we learned in Part I to a whole new level.

Parts I and II also focused on a more "traditional" approach to distributed programming. We used two different computers—one with code and the other to invoke methods. By doing so, we were able to harness the power of multiple computers to enhance our performance, reliability, and sometimes clarity. But this came at the cost of security, and the potential of having our great architecture become a tangled spider web of interdependence and poorly designed APIs.

Part III breaks from this "traditional" approach of distributed computing and looks at distributed message queues. The first section of Chapter 7, "Starling," provides a decent introduction to the concept of distributed message queues. If you are a newbie using distributed message queues, or you just don't know what one is, I highly recommend that you read the first section Chapter 7. It's not that long, and it might just help answer some of your questions upfront. However, if you are experienced with queues, you can probably just skip it and move on to the "good" stuff.

Distributed message queues are a great way to add distributed programming to your bag of tricks without the inherent security risks or potentially bad APIs. But you have to give up some flexibility, as you will see in the next chapters. If you keep an open mind, I'm sure you'll pull out a nugget or two that will instantly make your applications faster and easier to maintain.

CHAPTER 7

Starling

"Starling is a powerful but simple messaging server that enables reliable distributed queuing with an absolutely minimal overhead."[1] Originally developed by Twitter, Starling has become a mainstay in the Ruby community for distributed message queuing.

Now, before you quickly dismiss Starling because you have heard of Twitter's very famous performance issues, I ask that you still read this chapter. It talks a lot about what a distributed message queue is, how to use it, and lets you in on some of the mistakes Twitter made so that you don't make them yourself. Also, Twitter's performance issues weren't a result of Starling but of other rather poor technical and architectural issues. And who knows—you might really like Starling and end up using it. Remember that this book is less about the technologies discussed and more about the architecture and ideas these technologies represent. And Starling is no different.

What Is a Distributed Message Queue?

Distributed messaging is a bit different from what we have looked at so far in this book. We have discussed how to build systems where you can remotely invoke methods and how to pull remote code to your local system and run it, all in real time (see Figure 7-1). Distributed message queuing is quite different. You don't call a remote system and say, "Please invoke this method or action now." Instead, you send a message to the queue that at some point in the future will be picked up by a remote system (processor) and will then be acted on. If there are no messages, the processor keeps checking until it finds a message to act on. When a message is found, the processor processes it, and the cycle starts again. Figure 7-2 shows this flow in action.

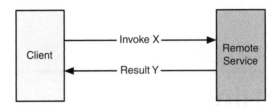

Figure 7-1   Typical invoke/respond distributed application call stack.

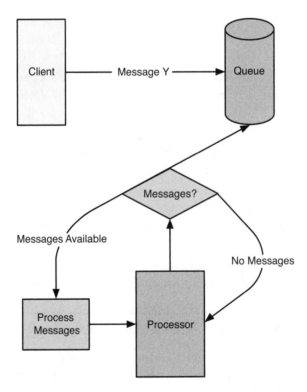

Figure 7-2   The typical flow of a distributed message queue.

Now that you have a basic understanding of what a distributed message queue is, why would you want to use one? To help answer that question, let's take a look at why Twitter wanted one.

Picture Twitter's application, if you can. Twitter has lots of people tweeting simultaneously. When a tweet comes in, it must be processed. When it is processed, the followers of the tweeters need to be notified of the new tweet. These notifications can range from emails to text messages to updating the tweeters page. If someone has a large number of followers, it can take several moments to generate and send those notifications. If Twitter were to try and do this in real time as new tweets arrived, then no new tweets would be able to get into the system because the servers would be too busy processing previous tweets. The system would fall down under the weight of it all. Enter the distributed message queue.

By using a distributed message queue, Twitter can process each tweet offline instead of when each one is submitted. This means that when tweets come in, the requests can be handled quickly. Later a processing server can come along, pick the tweets off the queue, and process them. This makes for a much more responsive and scalable system.

```ruby
# Example of queuing an incoming tweet:
def incoming_tweet(user, message)
  tweet = Tweet.create(:user => user, :message => message)
  starling.set('new_tweets', tweet.id)
end

# Example of processing queued tweets:
loop do
  tweet_id = starling.get('new_tweets')
  tweet = Tweet.find(tweet_id)
  # do notification of new tweets here...
end
```

Installation

Starling is installed using RubyGems:

```
$ gem install starling
```

Upon installation, you should see the following message:

```
Successfully installed starling-0.9.8
```

Getting Started with Starling

Starling is an interesting library. Instead of building everything from scratch, Blaine Cook and company decided to "speak" Memcached.[2] This means that they use the same protocols as a Memcached server. Because of this, any language or API that knows how to talk to Memcached can easily talk to Starling and make use of queues that have been created or are being managed by Starling. Please don't confuse this to mean that Starling uses Memcached—it just mimics its API as a means of convenience. There is a slight caveat to this, but I'll talk about that in just a little bit.

Starling comes with a binary to help get a server up and running quickly and easily. To see a list of options available to the Starling server, simply type the following into a terminal window:

```
$ starling --help
```

The results should be similar to the following:

```
Starling (0.9.8)

usage: starling [options...]
       starling --help
       starling --version
Configuration:
    -f, --config FILENAME      Config file (yaml) to load
    -q, --queue_path PATH      Path to store Starling queue logs
                               (default: /var/spool/starling)
Network:
    -h, --host HOST            Interface on which to listen
                                   (default: 127.0.0.1)

    -p, --port PORT            TCP port on which to listen
                                   (default: 22122)
Process:
    -d                         Run as a daemon.
    -P, --pid FILENAME         save PID in FILENAME when
                                   using -d option.
                               (default: /var/run/starling.pid)

    -u, --user USER            User to run as
    -g, --group GROUP          Group to run as
```

```
Logging:
    -L, --log [FILE]            Path to print debugging information.
    -l, --syslog CHANNEL        Write logs to the syslog instead
                                    of a log file.
    -v                          Increase logging verbosity
                                    (may be used multiple times).
    -t, --timeout [SECONDS]     Time in seconds before disconnecting
                                    inactive clients (0 to disable).
                                (default: 0)
Miscellaneous:
    -?, --help                  Display this usage information.
    -V, --version               Print version number and exit.
```

For our examples we can start a simple Starling server with the following command:

```
$ sudo starling
```

This should print something similar to the following:

```
I, [2009-05-13T18:26:54.289564 #42130]  INFO -- :
  Starling STARTUP on 127.0.0.1:22122
```

The server is now running. If you want to `daemonize` and create a complex server setup, I recommend using the `config` setting and creating a YAML[3] file to store these settings to make it easy to start/restart your server. The following sidebar contains more information.

Configuring Starling with YAML

If you are creating complex servers, it is probably best, and easiest, to use a YAML file to store those configurations. This makes it convenient to launch new servers or to restart existing ones. The Starling binary has a built-in flag for starting the server with a YAML file.

So what would a configuration YAML file look like? Something like this:

```
starling:
  port: 22122
  pid_file: /tmp/starling/starling.pid
  queue_path: /tmp/starling/spool
  timeout: 0
  logger: /tmp/starling/starling.log
  log_level: DEBUG
  daemonize: true
```

With our YAML file in place, we can start the Starling
server like this:

```
$ sudo starling --config config.yml
```

Now the Starling server is started as a daemonized service
with the options just listed. For more information about
each option, see the Starling documentation.

With our server now running, we can create a simple example to show that it is
working:

```
require 'rubygems'
require 'starling'

starling = Starling.new('127.0.0.1:22122')

10.times do |i|
  starling.set('my_queue', i)
  sleep(1)
end
```

Here we are creating a new instance of the Starling class, telling it what host
and port the Starling server is running on. After that we run a loop that sets the numbers 0 to 9 into a queue on the Starling server. We do that by calling the set method
on our Starling instance. The set method takes two parameters.[4] The first is the
name of the queue—in our case, my_queue. With Starling there is no need to formally

create a queue before you use it. The reason for this is that Starling will automatically create the queue for you, should it not exist. This makes for easy maintenance and set up. The downside to this is that if you mistype the name of the queue—either when setting messages into the queue or trying to get them out—you will never know because no exception will be thrown. This is something to keep in mind when debugging.

The second parameter to the set method is the object we want to store in the queue—in our case, a number from 0 to 9.

To retrieve our messages from the queue, we would write something like this:

```
require 'rubygems'
require 'starling'

starling = Starling.new('127.0.0.1:22122')

loop do
  puts starling.get('my_queue')
end
```

Again we create an instance of the Starling class, telling it on what host and port to find the server. After we have our instance, we simply create an infinite loop to continually keep looking for items in the queue. To retrieve an item from the queue, we call the get method and pass it the name of the queue from which we want to get our messages.

The get method works on a FIFO (first in, first out) system, popping the first message off the queue each time it is called. Because of this, we should see the following printed to the screen when we run our examples:

```
0
1
2
3
4
5
6
7
8
9
```

Using FIFO means that the first messages always take priority over newer messages that may arrive.

Remember that earlier I mentioned there was a caveat in regard to Starling implementing the Memcached API? Well, we have just seen in. If we were to set something into Memcached, it would overwrite whatever previous value had been there. This is not the case with Starling. Instead, when you call the set method with Starling, it actually appends the value to the end of the queue and does not overwrite it. This is a subtle difference but a rather important one to watch out for.

Flushing the Queue

An alternative to looping over the get method is to use the flush method. This provides a simple way to quickly access all messages in the specified queue. Let's look at a simple example:

```
require 'rubygems'
require 'starling'

starling = Starling.new('127.0.0.1:22122')

10.times do |i|
  starling.set('toilet', i)
end

starling.flush('toilet') do |message|
  puts message
end
```

This code produces the following output:

```
0
1
2
3
4
5
6
7
8
9
```

You can also call the `flush` method without a block, which causes the queue to simply be flushed without any processing being done on it.

One other important thing to note with the `flush` method is that it uses the `sizeof` method internally. So if ten messages are waiting, it calls the `get` method ten times. This means that if an eleventh message comes in during that time, it doesn't get processed as part of the original `flush` call.

You should know two more important things about the `get` method. The first is that after the `get` method returns an object to you, that object is no longer in the queue. This is important to know so that you handle exceptions properly. Take the following code, for example:

```
require 'rubygems'
require 'starling'

starling = Starling.new('127.0.0.1:22122')

starling.set('my_queue', 'Hello')
```

This code simply sets the word Hello into the queue. Now let's assume our processing class looks something like this:

```
require 'rubygems'
require 'starling'

starling = Starling.new('127.0.0.1:22122')

results = starling.get('my_queue')

results.flatten
```

When we run this code, we get the following error:

```
NoMethodError: undefined method 'flatten' for "Hello":String
```

I know this is a fairly contrived example, but it illustrates a good point. Our first set of code places a `String` in the queue, and the second piece of code expects an `Array`. Because our second piece of code gets the object from the queue and then raises an exception, if we were to run the same processing code again, we wouldn't find the object again in the queue. That's because the get method pops the message off the queue. Be careful to return objects to the queue if there is a problem. Here we have revised our processing code to fix the problem if it's a `NoMethodError`, or to simply return the object to the queue if another exception is raised:

```
require 'rubygems'
require 'starling'

starling = Starling.new('127.0.0.1:22122')

results = starling.get('my_queue')

begin
  results.flatten
rescue NoMethodError => e
  puts e.message
  starling.set('my_queue', [results])
rescue Exception => e
  starling.set('my_queue', results)
  raise e
end
```

This isn't the greatest bit of code, but you get the point. You need to be careful, or messages could very easily get lost due to a processing error.

That's the first thing you need to know about the get method. The second thing is that the get method blocks until something is returned. What does this mean? It means that when you call the get method it hangs execution of the thread until something is returned to it. For example, let's say nothing is placed into the queue for 5 minutes. The get method just sits there waiting for 5 minutes until something is available. The get method does not time out. Because of this, it is recommended that you have a dedicated script/thread to handle making calls to the get method.

"Hello World" the Starling Way

With our feet now firmly planted in the world of distributed queues and the basics of how Starling works, let's turn our attention to our familiar examples and see how Starling applies, if at all. First up is the obligatory "Hello World" example:

```
require 'rubygems'
require 'starling'

starling = Starling.new('127.0.0.1:22122')

starling.set('hello', 'Hello, World!')
```

This should seem quite familiar at this point. We create a new instance of the `Starling` class and tell it on what host and port to find the server. Then we call the `set` method, passing the "hello" as the name of the queue and our greeting, "Hello, World!", as the message.

Our processing code would look something like this:

```
require 'rubygems'
require 'starling'

starling = Starling.new('127.0.0.1:22122')

puts starling.get('hello')
```

When run it we see `Hello, World!` printed to the screen.

This is a pretty simple example. In most of our other examples we've had a nice `HelloWorld` class that we dealt with. Let's see how that works out with Starling. Let's start with the definition of our `HelloWorld` class:

```
class HelloWorld

  def say_hi
    'Hello, World!'
  end

end
```

Now let's add a `HelloWorld` instance to our queue:

```
require 'rubygems'
require 'starling'
require 'hello_world'

starling = Starling.new('127.0.0.1:22122')

starling.set('hello', HelloWorld.new)
```

Seems pretty straightforward. Now let's create our processing code:

```
require 'rubygems'
require 'starling'

starling = Starling.new('127.0.0.1:22122')

hello = starling.get('hello')

puts hello.say_hi
```

Again, this seems straightforward. We call the `get` method on our instance of the `Starling` class and ask it for the next message in the `hello` queue. We then get back our instance of the `HelloWorld` class and call the `say_hi` method on it. However, when we run this code we get the following error:

```
ArgumentError: undefined class/module HelloWorld
```

This error is similar to one we saw when we first sent a proprietary object across the wire with DRb. When we were dealing with DRb, we simply included the DRbUndumped module, and the problem went away. However, it is not that simple with Starling.

The DRbUndumped trick worked so well with DRb because we were using DRb to transport objects, and it has special hooks to deal with this problem. Starling, on the other hand, does not use DRb and does not give you a good way to handle this situation. The problem, if you remember, arises because the Ruby VM that set the object into the queue has the class definition for the `HelloWorld` class, but the Ruby VM getting the object from the queue does not have the class definition. So when the object is deserialized, there is no class definition to deserialize it into.

The only way to solve this problem is to require the class definition into all Ruby VMs that are expected to handle that class. This would mean our processing class would now have to look like this:

```
require 'rubygems'
require 'starling'
require 'hello_world'

starling = Starling.new('127.0.0.1:22122')

hello = starling.get('hello')

puts hello.say_hi
```

With the simple inclusion of `require 'hello_world'` we now have access to the `HelloWorld` class definition, and our code will now spit out the happy greeting "Hello, World!"

Building a Distributed Logger with Starling

Moving on with our examples, let's look at "Distributed Logger." This example is actually simple with Starling, because the very act of logging is simply sending the logger a message to log.

Writing a message to our distributed logger is similar to our other examples:

```
require 'rubygems'
require 'starling'

starling = Starling.new('127.0.0.1:22122')

starling.set('d-logger', 'Hello, World!')
starling.set('d-logger', 'Another Message')
```

On the logger side of things:

```
require 'rubygems'
require 'starling'
require 'logger'
```

```
starling = Starling.new('127.0.0.1:22122')

logger = Logger.new(STDOUT)

loop do
  message = starling.get('d-logger')
  logger.info(message)
end
```

Here we are creating our `Logger` instance. Then, in an infinite loop, we look for messages in our `d-logger` queue. When we find a message, we log it. Again, this sort of messaging is what Starling is designed for, and Starling excels at it. If you want to get clever, you could create more queues, one of each of the different levels of logging available, and write your messages to those particular queues instead of having all messages logged to the `info` method. I'll leave that up to you to play around with.

Persisted Queues

As mentioned earlier, Starling uses the Memcached protocol, which might beg the question, "Why not just use Memcached?" That's a great question. The answer is you could use Memcached instead of Starling, but you will lose several key features of Starling, including one very important feature—persisted queues.

When you shut down a Memcached server, you lose all of its contents. When you are trying to build a reliable queuing system, this is unacceptable. Starling solves this problem by persisting queues across server restarts. You can easily test this. First, place a message into the queue. Next, stop and restart the Starling server. Now try to retrieve the message from the queue. You'll see that the message is still there.

Constantly persisting messages does have the negative side effect of slowing down the queue slightly because it has to talk to its persistence mechanism. But this is a small price to pay for the reliability of being able to recall unsent messages after a system failure or restart.

Getting Starling Stats

Getting statistics for any system is extremely important in helping diagnose issues with your system and in helping fine-tune and refine the system. Starling gives you several tools to help with this.

The first is a simple binary, `starling_top`, that dumps a bunch of stats to your screen that look something like this:

```
bytes: 189
bytes_read: 3339
bytes_written: 3962
cmd_get: 115
cmd_set: 54
curr_connections: 1
curr_items: 15
get_hits: 39
get_misses: 76
limit_maxbytes: 0
pid: 42130
queue_hello_age: 14455
queue_hello_expired_items: 0
queue_hello_items: 1
queue_hello_logsize: 183
queue_hello_total_items: 7
queue_my_queue_age: 7043
queue_my_queue_expired_items: 0
queue_my_queue_items: 10
queue_my_queue_logsize: 16240310
queue_my_queue_total_items: 484503
rusage_system: 10.660000
rusage_user: 14.410000
time: 1242298907
total_connections: 51
total_items: 54
uptime: 63293
version: 0.9.8
```

Some of this information can be retrieved programmatically from Starling. Starling provides a method called `stats` that returns a `Hash` of `Hashes`. The keys to the first `Hash` are each of the Starling servers, and its value is a `Hash` containing key-value pairs for each of the available stats. We can re-create, mostly, the `starling_top` binary programmatically with the following code:

```
require 'rubygems'
require 'starling'
```

```
starling = Starling.new('127.0.0.1:22122')

all_stats = starling.stats

all_stats.each do |server, stats|
  puts "Server: #{server}"
  stats.each do |stat_name, stat_value|
    puts "#{stat_name}: #{stat_value}"
  end
end
```

This gives us output similar to the following:

```
Server: 127.0.0.1:22122
queue_my_queue_logsize: 16240310
queue_my_queue_total_items: 484503
get_hits: 39
bytes: 189
rusage_system: 11.13
pid: 42130
queue_my_queue_age: 7043
queue_hello_logsize: 183
queue_hello_total_items: 7
limit_maxbytes: 0
queue_my_queue_items: 10
queue_hello_expired_items: 0
time: 1242299849
queue_hello_items: 1
queue_hello_age: 14455
version: 0.9.8
bytes_written: 25304
total_items: 54
queue_my_queue_expired_items: 0
cmd_get: 115
total_connections: 58
curr_connections: 1
uptime: 64235
cmd_set: 54
rusage_user: 14.63
bytes_read: 3514
get_misses: 76
curr_items: 15
```

Being able to get this information programmatically is a great help. You can easily write scripts to monitor the health of your system and to take action if there is a problem.

You can also combine the `available_queues` and `sizeof` methods to get some basic stats:

```
require 'rubygems'
require 'starling'

starling = Starling.new('127.0.0.1:22122')

queues = starling.available_queues

queues.each do |queue|
  puts "#{queue} has #{starling.sizeof(queue)} messages."
end
```

This should yield a result similar to the following:

```
my_queue has 10 messages.
hello has 1 messages.
```

The `available_queues` method gives us an `Array` containing the names of all the queues that the server is currently aware of. The `sizeof` method takes the name of a queue and tells you how many messages it currently contains. If you pass in a queue that doesn't exist, the `sizeof` method simply returns 0.

The `sizeof` method has another trick up its sleeve. If you pass in `:all` to the method, it returns a `Hash` containing the names of each queue in the system and the number of messages currently in that queue. This means that the preceding example could be rewritten to look like this:

```
require 'rubygems'
require 'starling'

starling = Starling.new('127.0.0.1:22122')

queues = starling.sizeof(:all)

queues.each do |queue, size|
  puts "#{queue} has #{size} messages."
end
```

Conclusion

There is certainly no denying that Starling is a remarkably easy-to-use distributed message queue. That is why it has been so prominent in the Ruby community for several years. It is fast and effective. If Starling has a downside, it is that you have to constantly poll it to find out if any new messages need processing. Systems such as RabbitMQ allow you to subscribe to a queue that notifies you when a message is available for processing. We will talk about RabbitMQ in Chapter 8, "AMQP/RabbitMQ."

In addition to lacking a subscription/callback system, Starling lacks a few other nice-to-have features. But the lack of those features certainly does not stop Starling from being a great tool to add to your arsenal, especially if you want quick setup and ease of use.

Endnotes

1. http://github.com/starling/starling/tree/master

2. http://www.danga.com/memcached/

3. http://www.yaml.org/

4. This is not entirely accurate. The set method actually takes four parameters. The third parameter is how long, in seconds, you want the object to live. By default this is 0, meaning it will live forever. The last parameter is called raw. By default this value is false. When it is set to false, the object is marshaled before being placed into Memcached. If it is set to true, the object is not marshaled. There is a third variation on this. If you set the raw parameter to :yaml, the object is dumped to YAML before being sent to Memcached. This is useful if you plan on using other languages in addition to Ruby to access your queues.

CHAPTER 8

AMQP/RabbitMQ

In the preceding chapter on Starling, you learned about distributed message queues and how and when they can be advantageous to use. I also said that Starling has been a mainstay in the Ruby community for several years. Recently a new contender to the throne has arisen: RabbitMQ.[1] Here is what the developers of RabbitMQ have to say about it:

> "RabbitMQ is a complete and highly reliable Enterprise Messaging system. The RabbitMQ client libraries and broker daemon can be used together to create an AMQP network, or used individually to bring the benefits of RabbitMQ to established networks."

In short, they are saying that it is a distributed messaging queue, not too dissimilar from Starling, but it implements the AMQP[2] protocol instead of the Memcached protocol that Starling implemented.

It allows implementations of a few other interesting architectural designs that can prove to be useful in the world of distributed programming.

What Is AMQP?

AMQP stands for Advanced Message Queuing Protocol. AMQP is being designed as a common queuing protocol for enterprise systems to use. The protocol was designed by Cisco, Microsoft, Novell, and Red Hat, to name just a few. The goal of the project is to have a stable, fast, and reliable system that can be run on multiple environments and that is accessible from any language.

The AMQP website answers the questions of "why" and "what" quite nicely:

> *"Though many networking protocol needs have been addressed, a large gap exists in common guaranteed-delivery messaging middleware. AMQP fills that gap. AMQP enables complete interoperability for messaging middleware; both the networking protocol and the semantics of broker services are defined in AMQP."*

When working with an AMQP-compatible server, you should be aware of three main parts. The first is the exchange, which inspects the incoming message and finds the appropriate binding for it. The binding tells the exchange which message queue the message should be delivered to. Figure 8-1 shows this interaction.

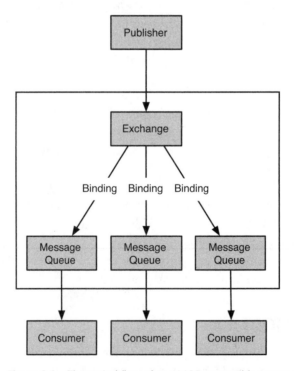

Figure 8-1   The typical flow of an AMQP-compatible server.

To help clarify what these different parts of the server do, the team developing AMQP use the example of an email system. This metaphor is quite nice and easy to understand:

- A message is analogous to an email message.

- A message queue is similar to that of an email mailbox for a particular email address.

- The exchange acts in much the same way that a mail transfer agent (MTA) would. It inspects the message and decides, based on routing keys and tables, to which message queue the message should be delivered. This is similar to how an MTA inspects the email and decides to which email mailbox it should be delivered based on things like the To: and Cc: address.

- A routing key is much like an email address attached to an email. It is important to note that domain information, like in an email address, is unnecessary, because all routing is done entirely internal to an AMQP server.

- A binding is like an entry in an MTA routing table.

Because this is just a high-level introduction to idea of the AMQP, I won't go into much more detail. If you are interested in knowing about the fundamentals of AMQP, I strongly encourage you to read the great specifications document posted on the AMQP site. It goes into much detail about the inner workings of the AMQP protocol to a level that isn't covered in this book.

Installation

Because AMQP is just a protocol, we need to install a server that implements that protocol. One of the leading servers that does just that is RabbitMQ, which has achieved quite a buzz in the Ruby community, despite not being written in Ruby. The reason for this is its speed, reliability, and ease of use.

Installation of RabbitMQ can be either quite simple or a bit difficult, depending on your platform. RabbitMQ is built using the Erlang language, so you need to make sure that it is installed before you try to install RabbitMQ. I won't go into detail about how to install RabbitMQ, because the process varies greatly for each environment, and relatively easy instructions can be found at http://www.rabbitmq.com/install. html.

Help with the Installation

When trying to get RabbitMQ installed and set up on my machine, I ran into a host of errors and turmoil. I ended up spending four hours trying to install it. After that, it was nearly impossible to get it to run.

The installation varies for each system, so I can't possibly document each one—nor do I want to. But let me tell you the issues that occurred on my Mac OS X machine, in the hopes that it may help you if you get stuck.

My biggest problem with the installation was that I had a previous installation of Erlang on my machine that I had built from source. I was trying to install RabbitMQ using MacPorts. When I tried to start RabbitMQ, using the start instructions on the RabbitMQ website, I got a big Erlang stack trace, and the server died.

To solve this problem, I uninstalled Erlang and RabbitMQ and then reinstalled them both using MacPorts. This time I successfully started the server.

Your mileage may vary with your installation, but this is what cleared things up for me.

After you have installed RabbitMQ, it is easy to get up and running in a Ruby environment. To use RabbitMQ with Ruby, we simply need to install the AMQP gem[3] using RubyGems:

```
$ gem install amqp
```

Upon installation you should see the following message:

```
Successfully installed amqp-0.6.0
```

"Hello World" the AMQP Way

After everything is installed and ready to go, we can start using RabbitMQ and the AMQP gem to build a highly robust and stable distributed message queue. First, though, we need to be sure to start the RabbitMQ server. Follow the instructions for your operating system on how to start the server. For Mac OS X this command should work:

```
$ sudo -H -u rabbitmq rabbitmq-server
```

On Mac OS X this results in something similar to the following being printed to the screen:

```
RabbitMQ 1.5.3 (AMQP 8-0)
Copyright (C) 2007-2009 LShift Ltd., Cohesive Financial Technologies
LLC., and Rabbit Technologies Ltd.
Licensed under the MPL.  See http://www.rabbitmq.com/

Logging to "/opt/local/var/log/rabbitmq/rabbit.log"
SASL logging to "/opt/local/var/log/rabbitmq/rabbit-sasl.log"

starting database             ...done
starting core processes       ...done
starting recovery             ...done
starting persister            ...done
starting guid generator       ...done
starting builtin applications ...done
starting TCP listeners        ...done

broker running
```

You need to have RabbitMQ running for each of the examples we will look at, but I highly recommend that you stop and restart the server before each set of examples. See the documentation for your operating system to learn how to stop and restart the server on your system. In production I recommend running it as a background daemon using the -detached option. I also recommend that you read the accompanying documentation for other configuration information.

Help with Stopping RabbitMQ

If you are running the server without the `-detached`
option, you should be able to kill the server by pressing
Ctrl-C. However, if you are running it in the background
with `-detached`, you should be able to stop it with the
following command:

```
$ sudo rabbitmqctl stop_app
```

When I first tried to run this command, I got the following
error:

```
Stopping node rabbit@macbates ...
Error: {badrpc,nodedown}
```

It turns out I was not running the server as the proper user.
I had been running the server with the following command:

```
$ sudo rabbitmq-server
```

It should have been the following:

```
$ sudo -H -u rabbitmq rabbitmq-server
```

The `-u` option allows the RabbitMQ server to run as the
`rabbitmq` user—which is, apparently, what the `rabbit-
mqctl` script is expecting it to be run as.

Documentation

One thing I always lack in the Ruby community is good
documentation. In part, that fact inspired this book. The
lack of good documentation surrounding `DRb` and `Rinda`
led to the birth of this book. In general, I have found that,
despite the relatively easy methods of documenting Ruby

code, RDoc, and RI, few people take the time to adequately document their code. Instead, they opt for the "It's self-documenting" fallback.

When I opened the AMQP gem, I expected to find more of the same. I am here to tell you that Aman Gupta, the lead developer of the gem, has done a great job of documenting it. I wish all libraries were this well documented. It would make everyone's lives easier if we had a good evolving set of documentation that traveled with the code we were using.

Although I go into some detail about the AMQP gem, what it has to offer, and some of the ways you can use it in your code, there is no substitute for the real thing. Please take a few minutes, open the RDoc for the gem, and give it a good read. The many options and ways to configure this gem can seriously impact your architecture decisions, and you need to understand them.

When you are done reading the RDoc, drop Aman a line via his GitHub page at http://github.com/tmm1/amqp, and tell him you appreciate his taking the time to write such great documentation.

You will know if your server is running when you try to run your code and you see an error message similar to this:

```
AMQP::Error: Could not connect to server 127.0.0.1:5672
```

With our RabbitMQ server now running, we can commence with our routine first exercise of saying, "Hello, World!". Let's start by publishing our "Hello, World!" message:

```
require 'rubygems'
require 'mq'
```

```
AMQP.start do
  queue = MQ.queue('hello_world_queue')

  queue.publish('Hello, World!')
end
```

Unlike most RubyGems, the AMQP gem breaks with the convention of using the name of the gem as the file you need to use the gem. It is for this reason that we require the file mq and not amqp. Although I applaud Aman on a lot of how the AMQP gem is written, this is certainly not one of them. I am a firm believer in using the gem name as the name of the required file, and not another file.

After obtaining the proper files, we can start using the AMQP gem. To get started we call the start method on the AMQP module. This method makes our connection for us. Because of that, the start method takes an optional Hash of options to allow for configuration. The options are as follows, along with their respective defaults:

```
{
  # Server Address:
  :host => '127.0.0.1',
  :port => 5672,

  # Login:
  :user => 'guest',
  :pass => 'guest',
  :vhost => '/',

  # Connection Timeout:
  :timeout => nil,

  # Logging:
  :logging => false
}
```

The other argument we need to pass to the start method is a block representing the code we want to run in the context of the AMQP server we just connected to. In this block we need to gain access to the queue we are looking for. The easiest way is to use the queue method of the MQ class, as we have done in our example.

The Magic Queue

You might be wondering where your queue comes from when you call the queue method. You didn't create a queue through any configuration, but the queue method returns a valid queue for you anyway.

The answer is simple. When you access a queue, if it doesn't already exist, it is created. This allows you to write simple code that requires less error handling. More important, it lets you get on with designing and building your application without having to worry about creating new configuration files, installing and running those files, and so on.

Beware, though—this does have a drawback. Should you mistype the name of the queue, you then will either be trying to place messages into the wrong queue, or you'll pull them out of the wrong queue. If you are placing messages into a queue named my_queue and you are trying to pull them out of a queue named myqueue, you will not receive any errors, and debugging can be time consuming and difficult. If you are having some issues, make sure to check this first—it could very well be a simple typo causing your problems.

One solution for this might be creating a wrapper class around your queue and using that to access it, like such:

```
class HelloWorldQueue < MQ::Queue

  class << self

    def queue(options = {})
      MQ.queue('hello_world', opts)
    end

  end

end
```

```
queue = HelloWorldQueue.queue
queue.publish('Hello, World!')

queue.pop do |msg|
  puts "#{Time.now}: #{msg}" if msg
  queue.pop
end
```

Another solution would be to use a configuration tool to
define the names of your queues, and then use that whenever you try to access a queue.

When we have the queue, we can call the publish method on it, passing it our
message that we want our consumer to retrieve.

Now, let's look at that consumer to see what we are dealing with:

```
require 'rubygems'
require 'mq'

AMQP.start do
  queue = MQ.queue('hello_world_queue')

  queue.pop do |msg|
    puts "#{Time.now}: #{msg}" if msg
    queue.pop
  end

end
```

Like our publisher, we need to call the start method on the AMQP module to
connect to our server. Then we can call the pop method on the queue to retrieve the
next message in the queue. We pass the pop method a block that we want to execute.

In our case we say that as long as the message we receive is not nil, print that
message to the screen. Once we have done that, we call the pop method again. We call
the pop method again to create an infinite loop that is continually pulling messages
off the queue. We do not need to pass it a block again, because it retains the block
information from the first time we called it.

Running this code should produce something similar to the following:

```
Sun May 24 23:03:39 -0400 2009: Hello, World!
```

Why Does the Publisher Code Never Exit?

If you are observant, you probably noticed that both the consumer and publisher code, when executed, seem to run in an infinite loop and never exit. This seems to be the correct behavior for the consumer, because we want it to run forever and constantly look for new messages. But why is the publisher doing the same thing?

The publisher code does not need to hang; we just coded it that way—but for a very good reason. When we call the start method on AMQP and pass it a block, that block is run inside a Thread that never exits. We could easily have rewritten our publisher code to look like this:

```
require 'rubygems'

require 'mq'

Thread.new { AMQP.start }

queue = MQ.queue('hello_world_queue')
queue.publish('Hello, World!')
```

When we call the start method without the block, it does not create a Thread for us. Instead, it binds to the Thread that starts it. To get the real benefits of AMQP, it needs to be run in a separate Thread, so we have wrapped it in a new Thread.

In fact, this is also how we would have rewritten the code had it been in a larger application, such as a web application, that we know will run forever.

So why didn't we write our code like that? The answer is simple, and it might surprise you. When you call the `publish` method, it delivers the message asynchronously. This means that, in our example, the message might not get delivered before the program exits.

To prevent that, I could have added a call to `sleep` to tell the application to pause for a second before it exits. But that wouldn't have made much sense in the context of the examples in this chapter.

I also could have written the publisher example like this:

```
require 'rubygems'

require 'mq'

thr = Thread.new { AMQP.start }

queue = MQ.queue('hello_world_queue')
queue.publish('Hello, World!')

thr.join
```

In this version of the example we tell the application to `join` the `Thread` we have created to the application. However, this prevents the application from exiting, which brings us back to the original problem with the sample code.

I chose to use the `start` method call with the block for the examples merely because it is cleaner and makes things a bit nicer to look at.

In earlier chapters we used a proprietary `HelloWorld` class that looked something like this:

```
class HelloWorld

  def say_hi
    'Hello, World!'
```

```
      end

    end
```

To use this proprietary `HelloWorld` class, you would think we could do something like the following for our publisher:

```
require 'rubygems'
require 'mq'
require 'hello_world'

AMQP.start do
  queue = MQ.queue('hello_world_queue')

  queue.publish(HelloWorld.new)
end
```

The only difference in our new version of the publisher is that, when we call the `publish` method on our queue, we are passing it an instance of our `HelloWorld` class, and not just a `String` representing our message.

Learning from our previous mistakes with trying to run proprietary classes in a separate Ruby VM, we need to be sure to include the `HelloWorld` class definition in our consumer. With that said, we would expect our consumer to look like the following:

```
require 'rubygems'
require 'mq'
require 'hello_world'

AMQP.start do
  queue = MQ.queue('hello_world_queue')

  queue.pop do |msg|
    if msg
      puts "#{Time.now}: #{msg.say_hi}"
      queue.pop
    else
      EM.add_timer(1) do
        queue.pop
      end
    end
  end

end
```

Here we retrieve our queue and call the `pop` method on it to start retrieving instances of our `HelloWorld` class. If we find an instance, we call the `say_hi` method on it and print it to the screen with the current time. If we don't find an instance, we call the `add_timer` method on the `EM` class that ships with the EventMachine[4] library. The `add_timer` method is similar to the `sleep` method found on `Kernel`. In essence, it says wait *n* seconds until you run what is contained in the block.

> ### EventMachine
>
> EventMachine is a C extension to Ruby that provides event-driven I/O using a design pattern known as the Reactor pattern.[5]
>
> EventMachine is designed with two goals in mind: high scalability and stability, and an easy API that allows developers to focus on application logic and not on the difficulties of high-performance multithreaded architectures.

Everything seems okay with our publisher and consumer, but when we try to run it, we receive the following error:

```
NoMethodError: undefined method 'say_hi' for
  "#<HelloWorld:0x10173a8>":String
```

Well, there is a good reason that AMQP returns a `String` instead of our instance of the `HelloWorld` class. When we publish a message to our queue using the `publish` method, the `to_s` method on that message is called to make sure that the message is a `String`. The reason for this is because RabbitMQ is not a Ruby-based library; AMQP needs to be able to consistently send "safe" messages to it that will easily read when they come back again. `String` is definitely the easiest way to achieve that goal.

So how do we get around this problem? The answer is pretty simple and not overly complex. We need to serialize our `HelloWorld` instance to a `String` before we call the `publish` method. Then, when we retrieve the message from the queue again, we need to deserialize it and reconstitute our `HelloWorld` instance.

Our publisher needs just a simple change to make its part of the equation work:

```
require 'rubygems'
require 'mq'
require 'hello_world'

AMQP.start do
  queue = MQ.queue('hello_world_queue')

  dumped_hw = Marshal.dump(HelloWorld.new)

  queue.publish(dumped_hw)
end
```

Notice that this time, when we call the `publish` method, we are passing it a variable called `dumped_hw`. This variable is the result of passing our `HelloWorld` instance into the `dump` method on the `Marshal` module. The `dump` method converts our `HelloWorld` instance into a serialized `String` format that can easily be reconstituted later by our consumer.

Now that we have serialized our `HelloWorld` instance in our publisher, we need to update our consumer code to deserialize it:

```
require 'rubygems'
require 'mq'
require 'hello_world'

AMQP.start do
  queue = MQ.queue('hello_world_queue')

  queue.pop do |msg|
    if msg
      hw = Marshal.load(msg)
      puts "#{Time.now}: #{hw.say_hi}"
      queue.pop
    else
      EM.add_timer(1) do
        queue.pop
      end
    end
  end

end
```

Now when we find a message waiting for us on our queue, we first pass it through the `load` method on the `Marshal` module to deserialize it into an instance of the `HelloWorld` class. With it safely reconstituted, we can now run this code and get the following output:

```
Sun May 24 22:31:02 -0400 2009: Hello, World!
```

Building a Distributed Logger with AMQP

Most of the other chapters in this book have had a section dedicated to the task of building a distributed logger. This chapter is no exception. The good news for you, the reader, is that the AMQP gem has thoughtfully included an `MQ::Logger` class to make this task easy for us to accomplish.

Our code to publish messages to the log is fairly straightforward:

```
require 'rubygems'
require 'mq'
require 'mq/logger'

AMQP.start do
  logger = MQ::Logger.new

  logger.debug "Hello, World!"

  logger.error NoMethodError.new('foo')
end
```

As you can see, using the `MQ::Logger` class is actually no different from using the regular `Logger` class that ships with Ruby. In fact, the examples that ship with the AMQP gem even go so far as to alias the standard Ruby `Logger` class to the `MQ::Logger` class. I don't know if I agree with that, but it does say something about how easy the class is to use, that it can be a drop-in replacement.

You might have noticed that in our example we call the `error` method on the `MQ::Logger` instance and pass it an instance of a `NoMethodError` exception class. You'll remember that earlier we talked about how if we want to put a "complex" Ruby object in a queue, we have to marshal it first, but here we are not doing that. We simply pass it the full instance of the object. We can do that here because the `MQ::Logger` class takes care of marshaling the messages sent to its logging methods so that they can easily be unmarshaled on the receiving end. This also helps maintain compatibility with the standard `Logger` that ships with Ruby.

Now let's look at our consumer code:

```
require 'rubygems'
require 'mq'

AMQP.start do

  queue = MQ.queue('logger')

  queue.pop do |msg|
    if msg
      msg = Marshal.load(msg)
      puts msg.inspect
      queue.pop
    else
      queue.pop
    end
  end

end
```

Not too much should be surprising when you look at this code. It is, in essence, the same code from our previous "Hello World" examples. There are really only two differences. The first one is that we are accessing a queue named `logger`. We did not explicitly set a queue name when we set up our `MQ::Logger` instance earlier, but as part of the initialization of that class, it automatically sets up the queue. Unfortunately, this queue name is hardcoded in the AMQP gem, so if you don't like the name, you have to learn to live with it. The second difference in the code is simply that we print the value returned by the `inspect` method of the `msg` object we get back from the queue, after we have unmarshaled it. The reason for this is nothing more than it is a quick way to nicely print a `Hash` to the screen, which is the object we receive from the queue.

When we run this code, we should see results similar to the following:

```
{:severity=>:debug, :timestamp=>Fri May 29 22:18:17 -0400 2009,
:msg=>"Hello, World!"}
{:severity=>:error, :timestamp=>Fri May 29 22:18:17 -0400 2009,
:msg=>{:type=>:exception, :message=>"foo", :backtrace=>nil,
:name=>:NoMethodError}}
```

That wasn't so bad, was it? Compared to some of the other hoops we have had to jump through in this book to get distributed loggers to work, that was relatively easy and straightforward. One note, though. Earlier in this chapter I made a great deal of fuss about how great the AMQP gem is documented, and that certainly is true—with the exception of the `MQ::Logger` class. It's a simple class, and its usage is pretty straightforward, but it would be nice to see some documentation around this class. Hopefully, Aman will document it soon.

> ### Quison
>
> Shortly before this book was published, a new library emerged called Quison. According to its author, Dan DeLeo, "Quison lives to make AMQP work with your web server, and make it easy." What does that statement actually mean?
>
> Well, according to Dan it means that a set of monkey patches set up the required callbacks and/or worker threads so that AMQP will work correctly with Passenger, Mongrel, and Thin. Quison apparently also creates a pool of connections to the AMQP server to increase performance.
>
> Although this library looks promising, it is still very green and probably needs more extensive testing before it's ready for prime-time production use. It is also possible that by the time you read these lines this library is either widely used or perhaps even rolled into the AMQP library (the latter being my hope).
>
> Either way, it is nice to see a thriving community growing around the AMQP specification.

Persisted AMQP Queues

When creating and using a queue, it is important to decide whether that queue needs to be persisted. If the RabbitMQ server is terminated or restarted, how important to you is it that the messages are delivered when that server comes back online? For example, it might not be that important to persist debugging messages, but it might be very important to persist new stock purchase requests that come in.

So with that in mind, let's briefly talk about how we can make our AMQP queues, and messages, persistent. First, I would like to point out that according to the documentation, persistent queues are slower than nonpersistent queues. This makes sense if you think about how a nonpersistent queue retains messages in memory, whereas a persistent queue has to write and read messages from disk. This is important to keep in mind when designing your queue.

With those few architectural concerns out of the way, let's look at our publisher for this example:

```ruby
require 'rubygems'
require 'mq'

AMQP.start do
  queue = MQ.queue('long_live_queues')

  10.times do |i|
    queue.publish("#{Time.now} - #{i}")
  end

  puts "Finished publishing"

end
```

This example is straightforward. We access the `long_live_queues` queue and write to it ten messages, each with the current time and a number. Now, let's run the publisher code. After we see the "Finished publishing" message, let's stop and restart our RabbitMQ server.

After the RabbitMQ server has restarted, let's run the following consumer:

```ruby
require 'rubygems'
require 'mq'

AMQP.start do

  queue = MQ.queue('long_live_queues')
```

```
queue.pop do |msg|
  puts msg if msg
  queue.pop
end

end
```

The consumer code runs, but we did not receive any messages to process. It just continues to loop without printing anything. Why is that? Well, to start with, we need to make the queue it set a persistent queue.

By default all queues are nonpersistent. This is because of the performance concerns mentioned earlier. To make a queue persistent, we simply have to pass it the :durable option the first time we create the queue. Let's see what our publisher would look like when we add this flag:

```
require 'rubygems'
require 'mq'

AMQP.start do

  queue = MQ.queue('long_live_queues', :durable => true)

  10.times do |i|
    puts i
    queue.publish("#{Time.now} - #{i}")
  end

  puts "Finished publishing"

end
```

When we call the queue method to retrieve the queue, we set the :durable flag to true. By default, this setting is false. So now we should have a persistent queue, right? Not quite. First we need to make a change to our consumer:

```
require 'rubygems'
require 'mq'

AMQP.start do
```

```
queue = MQ.queue('long_live_queues', :durable => true)

queue.pop do |msg|
  puts msg if msg
  queue.pop
end

end
```

In our consumer we also set the :durable flag to true. You might be wondering why our consumer must know whether the queue is persistent. That is a great question. The answer, according to the documentation, is that the first person to create a queue and set the :durable flag wins. This means that all subsequent calls that attempt to set this flag are ignored. Because of that, we don't know which might start the consumer or the publisher first, so we have to be careful and set the correct flags in both places. I am not a big fan of this architecture, but that's the way it is, so we just have to accept it and work with it.

Now if we were to run our publisher, and then restart the RabbitMQ server, and then run our consumer code, we would expect to see the ten messages printed to the consumer's screen. However, this does not happen. Why?

Our messages did not get persisted because we did not tell the queue to persist them when we published them. Confused? That's okay; it's a little confusing at first. We have declared that our queue is a persisted queue. This means that we are allowed to put persistent messages into that queue. It does not mean that all messages are persistent messages. We need to declare that when we publish the message itself.

To tell the queue to persist a particular message, we need to pass the :persistent flag to the publish method. Let's look at our publisher code again, this time with the :persistent flag set for our messages:

```
require 'rubygems'
require 'mq'

AMQP.start do

  queue = MQ.queue('long_live_queues', :durable => true)

  10.times do |i|
    puts i
```

```
        queue.publish("#{Time.now} - #{i}", :persistent => true)
    end

    puts "Finished publishing"

end
```

Now, if we were to run our publisher code, restart the RabbitMQ server, and then run our consumer code, we should see the following printed:

```
Sun May 31 21:42:03 -0400 2009 - 0
Sun May 31 21:42:03 -0400 2009 - 1
Sun May 31 21:42:03 -0400 2009 - 2
Sun May 31 21:42:03 -0400 2009 - 3
Sun May 31 21:42:03 -0400 2009 - 4
Sun May 31 21:42:03 -0400 2009 - 5
Sun May 31 21:42:03 -0400 2009 - 6
Sun May 31 21:42:03 -0400 2009 - 7
Sun May 31 21:42:03 -0400 2009 - 8
Sun May 31 21:42:03 -0400 2009 - 9
```

I know it seems a little strange to first have to declare the queue as being persistent and then have to declare each message on that queue as persistent for it to work. But that is how the system is architected. It would be nice to have a flag that can be set on the queue to tell it to always persist every message it receives, but currently that functionality does not exist.

If you are struggling to figure out when you might use a mix of persisted and non-persisted messages in a persisted queue, let me point you toward logging. It is usually mission-critical to log error- and fatal-level messages. However, debug messages could probably be lost on a server reboot, and most people wouldn't even notice. So when we would publish our log messages, we would set the :persistent flag to true for error and fatal messages, and probably not set it for the other log levels.

Subscribing to a Message Queue

In all our earlier examples, we used the pop method to retrieve messages from our queues. Although this method is straightforward and easy to understand, it is not the most direct way of getting these messages. I wanted you to understand the mechanics

of what happens in a queue. With that said, there is a much easier way of getting messages from a queue—the subscribe method.

The subscribe method is a method on the MQ::Queue class. When called, the
subscribe method registers a callback with the queue, telling it to call the attached
block whenever a message appears in the queue. Let's look at an example.

Let's say we want to write an application that waits for stock prices to get published and then prints them to the screen. In the past we would have written the consumer of this queue similar to this:

```ruby
require 'rubygems'
require 'mq'

AMQP.start do
  queue = MQ.queue('dow jones')

  queue.pop do |msg|
    if msg
      puts "#{Time.now}: #{msg}"
      queue.pop
    else
      EM.add_timer(1) do
        queue.pop
      end
    end
  end

end
```

Although this code works, it is a bit heavy-handed. For a start, it constantly polls
the queue, looking for new messages. Unfortunately, this can cause a heavy load on
the server if a lot of people are constantly polling, trying to get their stock prices. And
what about when the market is closed? Should we still keep pounding the queue, looking for changes?

A better approach is to subscribe to the queue and let the queue notify the consumers when a new message has been added to the queue. This is a much more efficient approach. So with that in mind, what would our consumer look like with this
new subscription approach?

```
require 'rubygems'
require 'mq'

AMQP.start do
  queue = MQ.queue('dow_jones')

  queue.subscribe do |header, msg|
    puts "#{Time.now}: #{msg}"
  end

end
```

As you can see, we simply call the `subscribe` method on our queue, and we are instantly notified of new messages that appear. The block that is passed into the `subscribe` method is run when a new message is delivered. The block yields two objects. The first object is an instance of `AMQP::Protocol::Header`. If we were to inspect this header, we would see information similar to the following:

```
#<AMQP::Protocol::Header:0x108b9c4 @size=12,
 @klass=AMQP::Protocol::Basic,
@properties={:delivery_tag=>141,
 :routing_key=>"dow jones", :redelivered=>false,
 :content_type=>"application/octet-stream",
 :consumer_tag=>"dow jones-321927405514", :exchange=>"",
 :priority=>0, :delivery_mode=>1}, @weight=0>
```

There is a lot of information here, some of which we will cover a bit later in this chapter. Other bits we won't look at. Either way, it is nice to know what information you can retrieve from this header.

The second object that is yielded to us from this block is the actual message from the queue. It should be noted, however, that if you ask the block to yield just one object, that object will be the message, not the header object.

For the sake of completeness, here is the publisher that goes along with this consumer:

```
require 'rubygems'
require 'mq'

AMQP.start do

  def price_change
```

```
    pc = rand(1000) / 100.0
    pc *= -1 if (rand(2) == 1)
    pc
  end

  stock_market = MQ.queue('dow_jones')

  stocks = {:appl => 100.0, :msft => 50.0}

  EM.add_periodic_timer(1) do
    stocks.each do |stock, price|
      price += price_change
      stocks[stock] = price
      stock_market.publish("#{stock}: #{price}")
    end
  end

end
```

We will expand on this code a bit in the next section, when we talk about topics. If we were to run both the consumer and the publisher, we would see output similar to the following:

```
Fri May 29 23:44:25 -0400 2009: appl: 95.59
Fri May 29 23:44:25 -0400 2009: msft: 58.52
Fri May 29 23:44:26 -0400 2009: appl: 88.58
Fri May 29 23:44:26 -0400 2009: msft: 53.49
Fri May 29 23:44:27 -0400 2009: appl: 98.37
Fri May 29 23:44:27 -0400 2009: msft: 57.82
Fri May 29 23:44:28 -0400 2009: appl: 91.78
Fri May 29 23:44:28 -0400 2009: msft: 66.81
Fri May 29 23:44:29 -0400 2009: appl: 94.18
Fri May 29 23:44:29 -0400 2009: msft: 57.89
Fri May 29 23:44:30 -0400 2009: appl: 94.78
Fri May 29 23:44:30 -0400 2009: msft: 58.42
```

Topic Queues

Up to this point we have been writing all messages to one big queue and hoping that our consumer is prepared to handle each of these messages. But what if we want to handle different types of messages within a single queue differently?

Let me explain what I mean with a simple example. Consider the idea of logging. We want to log all our messages to a single "logging" queue. That makes sense, because they are all logging messages. Normally we want to write all the messages to a log file. However, when we get an error- or fatal-level message, we also want to send an email to someone to alert him or her of the problem.

So how would we do that with a single queue? We could write an `if` statement that parses the log message and determines its level and then decides accordingly, or we could use the concept of a topic.

Topic queues allow us to effectively write all our messages to a single queue. But by adding a routing key to the message, we can then write what is basically a filtered queue on our consumer side.

When we talked earlier about subscribing to a queue, we built a simple system that published stock prices for a few different stocks and then a consumer that read those prices and printed them to the screen. What if we wanted to monitor a particular stock and get an alert if the price should change by more than 5%? We could write an `if` statement, or we could use the power of topic queues. Guess which one we will use in this section? If you guessed using the `if` statement approach, then that was a swing and a miss.

Let's start by making a simple adjustment to the stock publisher code we looked at earlier:

```
require 'rubygems'
require 'mq'

AMQP.start do

  def price_change
    pc = rand(1000) / 100.0
    pc *= -1 if (rand(2) == 1)
    pc
  end

  topic = MQ.topic('dow_jones')

  stocks = {:appl => 100.0, :msft => 50.0}

  EM.add_periodic_timer(1) do
    stocks.each do |stock, price|
      price += price_change
```

```
      stocks[stock] = price
      topic.publish(price, :key => "dow_jones.#{stock}")
   end
 end


 end
```

There is nothing new in this code, except for the line where we call the `publish` method. Notice that we are now passing in a flag called `:key` with the values `dow_jones.appl` and `dow_jones.msft`. Those values allow us to build our "custom" queue in the consumer code.

AMQP uses dot notation to associate topics with each other. By giving our messages a `:key` value of something like `dow_jones.appl`, we are saying that this message and topic, `appl`, are a subset of the `dow_jones` topic and should be treated as such.

Let's look at our consumer code, because that might help further explain what we are talking about:

```
require 'rubygems'
require 'mq'

AMQP.start do

  topic = MQ.topic('dow_jones')

  previous_price = nil

  appl_queue = MQ.queue('apple')
  appl_queue.bind(topic, :key => 'dow_jones.appl')
  appl_queue.subscribe do |header, msg|
    msg = msg.to_f
    previous_price = msg if previous_price.nil?
    diff = msg - previous_price
    diff *= -1 if diff < 0.0
    per = (diff / previous_price) * 100
    if per > 5.0
      puts "! Apple was: #{previous_price} now: #{msg} !"
    end
    previous_price = msg
  end
```

```
all_queue = MQ.queue('all stocks')
all_queue.bind(topic, :key => 'dow_jones.*')
all_queue.subscribe do |header, msg|
  puts "#{header.routing_key}:\t#{Time.now}: #{msg}"
end

end
```

At first glance this code might make our eyes go a bit crossed, but after we start looking at it, it is actually straightforward.

To kick things off, first we need to get the topic we want to deal with. In our case we are interested in the dow_jones topic, so we retrieve it with the following line:

```
topic = MQ.topic('dow_jones')
```

When we have the topic, we create a new queue for apple so that we can monitor its stock and be notified with an alert if its price fluctuates by more than 5%. That is done with the following line that you should be familiar with by now:

```
appl_queue = MQ.queue('apple')
```

The next line is where the secret sauce of topics comes in:

```
appl_queue.bind(topic, :key => 'dow_jones.appl')
```

With this line we are binding the dow_jones topic to the apple queue, but we are telling it to feed only the apple queue messages that have a key of dow_jones.appl. In essence, messages are now copied to the apple queue for it do with as it pleases. The original message stays in the dow_jones queue, waiting for someone else to come and claim it.

The rest of the code in the apple queue subscribe block just determines whether it is changed by more than 5%, and then it prints a message.

Moving on, we want to print all our messages. Again we create a new queue:

```
all_queue = MQ.queue('all stocks')
```

This time we are calling the queue all stocks. We want to bind that queue to the dow jones topic:

```
all_queue.bind(topic, :key => 'dow_jones.*')
```

Notice that this time we use the wildcard * to tell the topic to give us all messages that
are a subset of dow_jones.

If we were to run our publisher and our consumer, we should see something like
the following printed:

```
dow_jones.appl:    Sun May 31 22:57:24 -0400 2009: 113.86
dow_jones.msft:    Sun May 31 22:57:24 -0400 2009: 70.89
dow_jones.appl:    Sun May 31 22:57:25 -0400 2009: 109.15
dow_jones.msft:    Sun May 31 22:57:25 -0400 2009: 80.25
dow_jones.appl:    Sun May 31 22:57:26 -0400 2009: 110.98
dow_jones.msft:    Sun May 31 22:57:26 -0400 2009: 70.55
! Apple was: 110.98 now: 102.2 !
dow_jones.appl:    Sun May 31 22:57:28 -0400 2009: 102.2
dow_jones.msft:    Sun May 31 22:57:28 -0400 2009: 71.55
! Apple was: 102.2 now: 110.09 !
dow_jones.appl:    Sun May 31 22:57:29 -0400 2009: 110.09
dow_jones.msft:    Sun May 31 22:57:29 -0400 2009: 63.92
! Apple was: 110.09 now: 103.54 !
dow_jones.appl:    Sun May 31 22:57:30 -0400 2009: 103.54
dow_jones.msft:    Sun May 31 22:57:30 -0400 2009: 73.74
dow_jones.appl:    Sun May 31 22:57:31 -0400 2009: 108.66
dow_jones.msft:    Sun May 31 22:57:31 -0400 2009: 81.27
```

We could have just subscribed directly to the dow jones topic, but I wanted to
show you how to use the wildcard system built into topic queues. If the top-level topic
was stocks, and you had two subtopics, stocks.us.appl and stocks.us.msft,
you might then just want to show all the us stocks. The wildcard would be a great way
of doing just that. Figure 8-2 shows how different messages flow through a single topic
and end up in one or more different queues.

Definition: Exchange Versus Queue

If you have been looking through the documentation that
accompanies the AMQP gem, you might be a little confused by the difference between a queue and an exchange.

The difference between these two systems is subtle but
important. A queue is the end of the line for a message. To
return to an analogy from earlier in this chapter, a queue is

like a mailbox. It is the final place an email ends up in the system.

An exchange, on the other hand, can be thought of like a filter. You can tell the exchange, or filter, where messages should be sent. Because of this it is possible to send the same message to multiple queues to be acted on.

When we set up a topic, for example, we are actually setting up an exchange with a particular filter attached to it. Later, when we create a queue to handle messages that meet a specific filter, we bind the queue to that topic so that the filter is applied and we see only the messages we want to see.

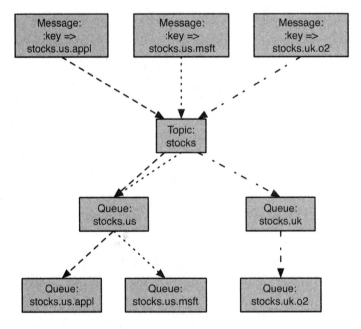

Figure 8-2 Different messages flow through a topic and end up in one or more queues.

Fanout Queues

A moment ago, when we discussed queues, we mentioned a style of queue known as a *direct queue*. This means that when we place a message on a queue, that message can be consumed only by direct access to that queue. This is the most straightforward, and common, type of queue. If you wanted several consumers to operate independently on a message, you were out of luck, because it was a shared queue.

Topic queues allow us to create filtered queues on-the-fly and manipulate the messages on those queues in a safe manner, because each filtered queue receives its own copy of the message. They also have the disadvantage of being more complicated; therefore, they are slower than a direct queue. Because of that, they are overkill for the simple task of creating a queue that allows multiple consumers to work on each message safely and independently of each other.

A third type of queue is called *fanout*. Fanout queues are a hybrid of sorts between direct and topic queues. They allow us to send a message to a single destination and allow that message to then be copied into multiple receiving queues. Once in each of those queues the messages can be operated on independently. Fanout allows us to perform $1:n$-style communication quickly and easily.

The caveat about using fanout with AMQP, and the big differentiator with topics, is that unlike with topics, you cannot filter out messages from the queue. With topics we can bind to a small subset of the messages in the queue. With fanout, our queues receive all messages that are placed in the original queue. This sounds an awful lot like the queues we discussed at the beginning of the chapter. The big difference between those queues and fanout queues is that each queue that is bound to the fanout queue gets its own copy of the message; it is not just popped off the top of the queue, as we have seen earlier. Figure 8-3 illustrates this point quite nicely.

Let's look at an example of how to use fanout queues with AMQP. In our example we want to write simple log messages to the queue and have them set to three log servers. These servers are there as redundancy. If one goes down, two servers are still available to write our logs for us. I know this is a fairly contrived example, but it works well enough for our purposes.

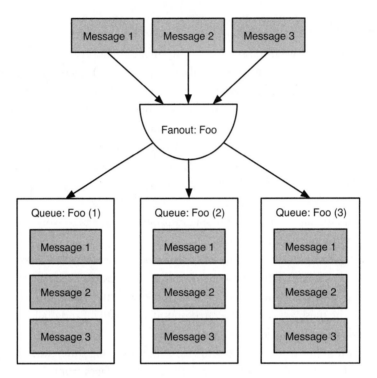

Figure 8-3   A fanout queue places a copy of each message
into each queues that is bound to the queue.

Building our publisher code to write to a fanout queue is not that different from
some of our other queues:

```
require 'rubygems'
require 'mq'

AMQP.start do

  logger = MQ.fanout('logger')

  logger.publish('log message #1')
  logger.publish('log message #2')
  logger.publish('log message #3')

end
```

In our publisher code, where we would normally call the `queue` method on `MQ`, we instead call the `fanout` method, giving it a name for the fanout queue. We then publish a few messages to it as normal.

On the consumer side of things, handling fanout queues is not much different from topics:

```ruby
require 'rubygems'
require 'mq'

AMQP.start do

  log_server_1 = MQ.queue('log server #1')
  log_server_1.bind(MQ.fanout('logger')).subscribe do |msg|
    puts "Log Server #1: #{msg}"
  end

  log_server_2 = MQ.queue('log server #2')
  log_server_2.bind(MQ.fanout('logger')).subscribe do |msg|
    puts "Log Server #2: #{msg}"
  end

  log_server_3 = MQ.queue('log server #3')
  log_server_3.bind(MQ.fanout('logger')).subscribe do |msg|
    puts "Log Server #3: #{msg}"
  end

end
```

This code should not look too different from our earlier topic examples. First we create a new queue to allow us to get a copy of the messages:

```ruby
log_server_1 = MQ.queue('log server #1')
```

We then bind that queue to the fanout queue and subscribe to the resulting queue:

```ruby
log_server_1.bind(MQ.fanout('logger')).subscribe
```

After we have bound the new queue and the fanout queue, the `subscribe` method, as mentioned earlier, takes a block that yields a message for us to manipulate as we please.

Unbinding

When we talked about topics and fanout queues, we discussed binding a queue to either a topic or fanout queue. But what happens if we want to remove that binding?

Why would we want to remove the binding between a queue and, let's say, a topic? Perhaps you just want to dip into the queue to do some debugging, or you want to take a pulse point, or perhaps you want to add extra horsepower during a heavy load time and decrease the number of consumers you have when the server load diminishes.

Whatever your reason for wanting to remove that binding, it is nice to know that this is very easy to do:

```
my_queue.unbind(MQ.topic("some_topic"))
```

The unbind method takes the same input that the bind method does—the queue you originally bound the current queue to.

Conclusion

The AMQP gem, protocol, and RabbitMQ are a powerful combination. This chapter has only touched on what they can do. These systems have proven to be stable, fast, and, as you've seen, easy to use. Because of these traits, AMQP and RabbitMQ have quickly risen to the top of the list when it comes to distributed message queuing systems.

I have mentioned several times in this chapter that the documentation that comes bundled with the AMQP gem is superb, but it deserves another mention here. Although I have outlined and given you brief examples of each of the highlights of this gem, it is important to know all the different options that are available for each of the methods and queues. Please take a good look at the documentation. It will definitely save you time and make your systems more stable, secure, and reliable.

Endnotes

1. http://www.rabbitmq.com/

2. http://www.amqp.org

3. http://github.com/tmm1/amqp/tree/master

4. http://rubyeventmachine.com

5. http://en.wikipedia.org/wiki/Reactor_pattern

PART IV
Distributed Programming with Ruby on Rails

When I came up with the idea for this book, I intended to make it strictly about "pure" Ruby. I had no intention of including any chapters that were specific to Ruby on Rails. However, after thinking about it, I realized it would be hard not to include the next couple of chapters. They focus on tools that work only within a Ruby on Rails environment, but they are so helpful that I would be remiss if I did not include them. They also demonstrate a few interesting architectural points worth discussing.

If you use Ruby on Rails, there is no reason for you not to read this part of the book. The tools in this part can help your Ruby on Rails applications scale and be more efficient and easier to code. You might already know about these tools, but I am convinced that I have written about aspects of the tool you probably don't know about. Or perhaps you thought the tool was doing something one way, when in fact it does it the opposite way. Understanding your tools better can help you write better code, which, in turn, makes for a better and more stable system.

Even if you don't use Ruby on Rails daily (some people who use Ruby don't use Ruby on Rails at all), I still recommend that you read this part of the book. You might find inspiration to write a "pure" Ruby port of these tools. Or you might contribute to them so that they can be used with your favorite Ruby framework. Or you might find a good reason buried in there to start using Ruby on Rails.

CHAPTER 9

BackgrounDRb

I started developing Ruby on Rails apps in late 2005. Rails was still pre-1.0 and had a lot of rough edges. One of those edges was the fact that it was single-threaded. I was willing to look past that minor limitation, at least for a little while, because I had just come from writing these enormous Java/JSP/Struts apps. Writing applications with Rails, even with its flaws, was like coding heaven compared to the Java world I had just come from. I assumed (and you know what happens when you do that) the ability to run Rails in a multithreaded environment would come with the 1.0 release.

Well, the 1.0 release came and went with no multithreaded support. This single-threaded limitation was really starting to become a problem—not only for me, but for a lot of people in the community. If you were doing a file upload, or some other hefty task, Rails would just sit there queuing up requests behind it, because it did not allow multiple threads, or processes, to be run so that you could handle all your requests.

I know I wasn't alone in my desire to offload heavy tasks to the background, because in 2006, Ezra Zygmuntowicz released the first version of BackgrounDRb.[1] BackgrounDRb is now being maintained by Hemant Kumar.[2]

The goal of BackgrounDRb was to have an easy-to-use mechanism to send these tasks to an alternative process so that they could be processed asynchronously from the main application process. Ezra chose DRb as the mechanism for passing off these tasks to the other process. This chapter looks at how to use this plugin for Ruby on Rails to perform these hefty tasks.

Installation

Before we jump into installing and configuring BackgrounDRb, let me state that I'm assuming you are already familiar with Ruby on Rails, its structure and layout, what a Rails plugin is, and other such generalities.

BackgrounDRb is installed as a plugin for Ruby on Rails. However, before we can install the plugin, we must install a few dependencies for it. BackgrounDRb requires two gems, in addition to Rails, to be installed first:

```
$ gem install chronic packet
```

That should install the prerequisite gems we need:

```
Successfully installed chronic-0.2.3
Successfully installed packet-0.1.15
```

With our gems now installed, let's create a new Rails project to work with:

```
$ rails bdrb
```

This spouts a bunch of Rails code-generation statements that I don't think I need to reproduce here. Most important, it creates a new directory called bdrb. Make sure you are in that directory from this point on. Now let's install the plugin:

```
$ ruby script/plugin install git://github.com/gnufied/backgroundrb.git
```

This creates a lot of files in our RAILS_ROOT/vendor/plugins/backgroundrb folder. Now that we have the plugin installed, we need to create the necessary database tables so that BackgrounDRb can do its thing. We can create and run the migrations we need by running the following Rake tasks:

```
$ rake backgroundrb:setup
$ rake db:migrate
```

You should see, among some other output, the following:

```
==  CreateBackgroundrbQueueTable: migrating
===================================
  -- create_table(:bdrb_job_queues)
     -> 0.0062s
  ==  CreateBackgroundrbQueueTable: migrated (0.0066s)
=========================
```

This tells us that the migration has been generated and run and has created a table named bdrb_job_queues.

Offloading Slow Tasks with BackgrounDRb

Thankfully we have fully installed BackgrounDRb into an application, and here is why. We have an application that creates widgets for us. The problem is that widget creation takes 30 seconds. When we try to create a widget via the web browser, it times out because it takes too long. Hopefully BackgrounDRb can solve our problem.

Let's take a step back and look at what we did to get ourselves into this situation. First we created our scaffolded model and controller with the following command:

```
$ ruby script/generate scaffold widget name:string body:text
$ rake db:migrate
```

Then in our model we added a before_save callback to do some essential processing:

```
class Widget < ActiveRecord::Base

  before_save :some_stupid_slow_processing

  private
  def some_stupid_slow_processing
    sleep(30)
  end

end
```

The create action method in our WidgetsController class looks like this:

```
def create
  @widget = Widget.new(params[:widget])
  if @widget.save
    flash[:notice] = 'Widget was successfully created.'
    redirect_to(@widget)
  else
    render :action => "new"
  end
end
```

If we were to create a new widget with our current code and look in the log file, we would see something similar to the following:

```
Completed in 30050ms (DB: 1)
```

As you can see, the request took over 30 seconds to complete. This is unacceptable in the real world. We can't have end users waiting for 30 seconds to create a new widget. Perhaps it would be better to push this task to the background and let the user know that we will be building his new widget and will let him know when it's ready.

Now that we understand the problem, how do we solve it? Let's take a look at how we can use BackgrounDRb to help.

BackgrounDRb has a concept called workers. These workers, well, do the work. We create a new worker class for each type of processing we want to do. Each worker has a method or series of methods that we can call asynchronously and pass parameters to that will eventually perform the processing offline. Later a background service will process each of those tasks and perform them. The application calls and passes parameters to these asynchronous background methods through DRb.

In our case we want to create a worker that will create our widgets for us. Thankfully BackgrounDRb has a built-in Rails generator to help us quickly create these new workers:

```
$ ruby script/generate worker widget
```

This command should output the following:

```
exists  lib/workers/
create  lib/workers/widget_worker_worker.rb
```

If we open widget_worker.rb, we see a class definition that looks like this:

```
class WidgetWorker < BackgrounDRb::MetaWorker

  set_worker_name :widget_worker

  def create(args = nil)
    # this method is called when worker
    # is loaded for the first time.
  end

end
```

Let's examine what our base worker class looks like. First, notice that `Widget-Worker` extends `BackgrounDRb::MetaWorker`, which handles almost all of the heavy lifting in terms of connecting to the background `DRb` service and running the asynchronous methods. Next we notice that we are calling a class method, `set_worker_name`, and passing it the value of `:widget_worker`. This is done so that we can easily identify the worker later in our code. At no point in our code will we explicitly instantiate an instance of `WidgetWorker`. Instead, we will use a `MiddleMan` class and give it the name of the worker we are interested in calling. But we don't want to get ahead of ourselves, so we will get to that shortly.

Finally, we have a method called `create`. The `create` method is called when the `WidgetWorker` is first initialized. This is similar to the `initialize` method we are used to in Ruby. You can use this method to configure variables and other items necessary for a successful worker instance. Because this method is called only once, it is not a good place for us to put our code to create new widgets. However, just so that we can see the life span of our `WidgetWorker` class, let's put a log statement in the `create` method so that we can see that it does in fact get called only once:

```
def create(args = nil)
  logger.debug "We have just created a new WidgetWorker!"
end
```

So if the `create` method is not a good place for us to place our new widget-creation code, where should we place it? Let's create a new method called `create_new_widget` and place it in there:

```
def create_new_widget(options = {})
  logger.debug "We need to create a new widget: #{options.inspect}"
  widget = Widget.create(options)
  logger.debug "We created widget: #{options.inspect}"
end
```

Our `create_new_widget` method takes a `Hash` of options that we can then pass to the built-in Rails method `create` on our `Widget` class. That is our unfortunate method that takes a whole 30 seconds to complete. I've added a few log statements to the method to help illustrate the flow through this method. So with these changes our `WidgetWorker` class now looks like this:

```
class WidgetWorker < BackgrounDRb::MetaWorker

  set_worker_name :widget_worker

  def create(args = nil)
    logger.debug "We have just created a new WidgetWorker!"
  end

  def create_new_widget(options = {})
    logger.debug "We need to create a new widget: #{options.inspect}"
    widget = Widget.create(options)
    logger.debug "We created widget: #{options.inspect}"
  end

end
```

We have created our worker class, `WidgetWorker`, which will handle the offline, asynchronous creation of our new widgets. But how do we call this code and tell it to do just that? We must change the `create` action in the `WidgetsController` class. We should update it to look like this:

```
def create
  widget_worker = MiddleMan.worker(:widget_worker)
  result = widget_worker.async_create_new_widget(:arg =>
params[:widget])
  if result == 'ok'
    msg = 'We are creating your widget. Please check back shortly.'
    flash[:notice] = msg
    redirect_to(widgets_url)
  else
    @widget = Widget.new(params[:widget])
    msg = 'There was an error creating your widget. Please try again
later.'
    flash[:error] = msg
    render(:action => 'new')
  end
end
```

This is quite a big change from our original `create` action. Let's work through it so that you understand what is happening. First we make a call to that mysterious `MiddleMan` class I referred to earlier. The `MiddleMan` class does just what its name says—it acts as a middleman between your application and the BackgrounDRb server.

Without it you would have to write a lot of code to make those connections. On the `MiddleMan` class we call the `worker` method and pass it the name of the worker we are looking for. In our case we are looking for `:widget_worker`. The `worker` method looks up a reference to our `WidgetWorker` and returns it to us so that we can interact with it. With that said, we don't get back an actual instance of our worker class. Instead, we get a proxy class that mimics the worker class. If we were to call the `inspect` method on our `widget_worker` variable, we would see something like the following:

```
#<BackgroundDRb::RailsWorkerProxy:0x1f2a23c
@middle_man=#<BackgroundDRb::ClusterConnection:0x2323c58
@backend_connections=[#<BackgroundDRb::Connection:0x22f0d08
@mutex=#<Mutex:0x22f0c04>,
@cluster_conn=#<BackgroundDRb::ClusterConnection:0x2323c58 ...>,
@server_port=11006, @connection=nil, @server_ip="0.0.0.0",
@connection_status=true>], @request_count=31,
@bdrb_servers=[#<struct #<Class:0x22f135c> ip="0.0.0.0",
port=11006>], @round_robin=[], @last_polled_time=Wed Jul 15
22:32:33 -0400 2009, @disconnected_connections={}>,
@worker_name=:widget_worker, @worker_key=nil, @tried_connections=[]>
```

We are actually returned an instance of a class called `BackgroundDRb::RailsWorkerProxy` and not `WidgetWorker`, as you might have thought. It is on this proxy that we will register a call to our `create_new_widget` method, passing in the `Hash` that represents the widget we want created. This proxy then generates a message and places it on a queue over `DRb` so that a background process can pop that message off the queue and process it for us. We create that message like this:

```
result = widget_worker.async_create_new_widget(:arg =>
params[:widget])
```

What Happens if No Worker Exists?

We have seen that when we call the `worker` method on the `MiddleMan` class, we are returned a `BackgroundDRb::RailsWorkerProxy` instance and not an instance of the actual worker class we have written. What happens if the worker we request does not exist? Let's see.

First, let's try to find a worker that does not exist:

```
ww = MiddleMan.worker(:i_do_not_exist)
```

This returns successfully. We get another instance of `Back-grounDRb::RailsWorkerProxy`. I would have expected this to either return `nil` or raise an exception, but it doesn't. The reason, as I understand it, is that the background process that is performing the tasks may or may not have the worker the application is requesting. The only way to find out is to make a remote method call and ask. But because that is somewhat expensive, it is just assumed that the worker you requested exists.

If we print the `inspect` method on our nonexistent worker, we see that it looks similar to the worker we retrieved earlier in the chapter:

```
#<BackgroundDRb::RailsWorkerProxy:0x1f40384
 @middle_man=#<BackgroundDRb::ClusterConnection:
 0x2323c58
 @backend_connections=[#<BackgroundDRb::
 Connection:0x22f0d08
 @mutex=#<Mutex:0x22f0c04>,
 @cluster_conn=#<BackgroundDRb::ClusterConnection:
 0x2323c58
 ...>, @server_port=11006, @server_ip="0.0.0.0",
 @connection_status=true>], @request_count=1,
 @bdrb_servers=[#<struct #<Class:0x22f135c>
 ip="0.0.0.0",
 port=11006>], @round_robin=[0], @last_polled_time=Wed
 Jul 15 23:28:30 -0400 2009,
 @disconnected_connections={}>,
 @worker_name=:i_do_not_exist, @worker_key=nil,
 @tried_connections=[]>
```

If we were to try to call a method on our nonexistent worker, we would be returned a `nil` instead of our successful status of `ok`.

The moral of this story is to always be sure to check the return status and handle it appropriately.

You can see that on our `widget_worker` variable we call a method we have never seen before, `async_create_new_widget`. This type of method is sometimes called a "magic" method. It's "magic" because it does not exist anywhere in the source code. `BackgrounDRb::RailsWorkerProxy` captures calls to methods that do not exist on it and interprets them as messages that need to be created on the queue. So why do we append `async_` to our `create_new_widget` method name? Well, by doing so we are telling BackgrounDRb that the `create_new_widget` method should be processed asynchronously and not inline. We also could have called the `create_new_widget` method on the proxy class, but that would have had the unfortunate downside of taking 30 seconds to process.

When we call our "magic" `async_create_new_widget` method, we pass in a `Hash` of options. The option we are most interested in, at least at this point, is `:arg`. The value of the `:arg` option is passed into the `create_new_widget` method on the `WidgetWorker` class.

When we call the `async_create_new_widget` method, we are returned a result code. If we get a result code of `ok`, we know that our message has been received successfully, and we can let the end user know too. It is worth pointing out that this status does not mean that our new widget has been successfully created. It simply means that the message was successfully received, stating that we want to call the `create_new_widget` method on the `WidgetWorker` class with a certain set of parameters.

With an `ok` result status we create a nice flash message letting the end user know that we are working on creating her widget and that it will be ready shortly. We then redirect the user to the widgets index page. If the result status is anything but `ok`, we return the end user to the widget creation screen. We present her with a message telling her that a problem has occurred and that she should try again later.

Oops! Something Went Wrong!

What happens if our background process fails and we never create the new widget? And how do we know that an error occurred?

Unfortunately, there is no built-in way to find out the answers to these questions with BackgrounDRb. You most likely would need another process that runs periodically to check on the status of these tasks. Or you would use a

> service, such as Hoptoad, that captures exceptions for you
> and lets you know when an error occurs.
>
> This is definitely a downside of BackgrounDRb and an area
> where competitors, such as Delayed Job,[3] have the upper
> hand.

Why don't we run this and try it out? Before we fire up our Rails application, we need to start a BackgrounDRb server:

```
$ ruby script/backgroundrb start
```

You should see the following:

```
Starting BackgrounDRb ....
```

Then the console returns to you. We can monitor the logging statements we put in our code by tailing the log file that BackgrounDRb creates for you:

```
$ tail -f log/backgroundrb_11006.log
```

You should immediately see our first logging statement get printed:

```
We have just created a new WidgetWorker!
```

Now let's start our application:

```
$ ruby script/server
```

Now let's navigate to http://localhost:3000/widgets. We should be presented with no widgets, so let's create one. Click the "New widget" link or go to http://localhost:3000/widgets/new. Give your widget a name and a body, and click the Create button. You should be taken back to the widgets index page and shown the following pleasant message:

```
We are creating your widget. Please check back shortly.
```

You should notice that the widget you just submitted is not listed on the page. Now if you go back and look at the log file we were tailing, you should see something like the following:

```
We need to create a new widget: {"name"=>"My Special Widget",
  "body"=>"This is my super cool new widget."}
```

Then, about 30 seconds later, you should see the following message:

```
We created widget: {"name"=>"My Special Widget", "body"=>"This is
  my super cool new widget."}
```

If you refresh the widgets index page, you will see your widget listed on the page. Congratulations! You have built a new worker, configured it, and updated your code to call your asynchronous method in your worker.

Configuring BackgrounDRb

Now that we have managed to sort out our slow-widget-creation problem, let's take a look at how we can configure BackgrounDRb. When we ran the `backgroundrb:setup` Rake task, one of the files that was generated was named backgroundrb.yml in the config directory of our Rails project. If we were to open this file, we would see the following configuration settings:

```
---
:backgroundrb:
  :ip: 0.0.0.0
  :port: 11006
```

This is the most basic configuration that BackgrounDRb needs to run. As you can probably guess from the settings, this configuration binds the BackgrounDRb process to 0.0.0.0:11006. However, this is not where the configuration of BackgrounDRb ends. A `backgroundrb.yml` file that has all its configuration parameters listed would look something like this:

```
---
:backgroundrb:
  :ip: 0.0.0.0
  :port: 11006
  :environment: production
  :debug_log: true
  :log: foreground
  :persistent_disabled: false
  :persistent_delay: 10

:client: "10.0.0.1:11006,10.0.0.2:11007"
```

Let's look at each of these configuration settings. We've already seen the `:ip` and `:port` settings, so we can skip those. The `:environment` setting tells BackgrounDRb which Rails environment to run in. The default for the `:environment` setting is `development`.

The `:debug_log` setting tells BackgrounDRb whether to write debug statements to a separate log file. By default this setting is `true`. Here is an example of what you would find in the debug log:

```
Invalid worker with name i_do_not_exist and key
/usr/local/lib/ruby/gems/1.8/gems/packet-0.1.15/lib/packet/
packet_connection.rb:52:in 'ask_worker'
/Users/markbates/bdrb/vendor/plugins/backgroundrb/server/lib/
master_worker.rb:159:in 'method_invoke'
/Users/markbates/bdrb/vendor/plugins/backgroundrb/server/lib/
master_worker.rb:42:in 'receive_data'
/usr/local/lib/ruby/gems/1.8/gems/packet-0.1.15/lib/packet/
packet_parser.rb:44:in 'extract'
/usr/local/lib/ruby/gems/1.8/gems/packet-0.1.15/lib/packet/
packet_parser.rb:26:in 'loop'
/usr/local/lib/ruby/gems/1.8/gems/packet-0.1.15/lib/packet/
packet_parser.rb:26:in 'extract'
/Users/markbates/bdrb/vendor/plugins/backgroundrb/server/lib/
master_worker.rb:32:in 'receive_data'
...
```

The `:log` setting tells BackgrounDRb where to log to. The default is to write to a log file in the log directory, where the naming scheme is `backgroundrb_port.log`. You can also set this to `foreground`, which writes log statements to STDOUT.

The `:persistent_disabled` setting disables the persistent storing of tasks in the database. The advantage of turning off persistence, as in all other queue mechanisms, is speed. Without having to persist tasks to a database, file, or other storage, the system performs at a much faster rate. The disadvantage, however, is that should some unforeseen incident occur and your BackgrounDRb processes die and need to be restarted, you lose any tasks that were waiting in the queue to be processed. This is definitely a business choice you need to make. There may be times when losing these tasks is perfectly acceptable, and other times when it is not.

The `:persistent_delay` setting tells BackgrounDRb how often, in seconds, it should check the database for new tasks to process. The default setting is 5 seconds. You need to fine-tune this setting to better match your environment. If you make it too often, you will process more often and therefore will create a heavier load on your systems. If you make it too seldom, the latency of processing these tasks can become quite noticeable to your end users.

The last setting we see is the :client setting. This is a comma-separated list of BackgroundDRb servers you have running. The point is to create clusters of BackgroundDRb servers that can have the load of tasks spread among them. BackgroundDRb uses round-robin[4] to pass tasks to each of the BackgroundDRb servers listed. If a server stops responding, BackgroundDRb stops sending tasks to that server until that server comes back online.

Persisting BackgrounDRb Tasks

We originally solved our slow-creating widget using an asynchronous background process that built the widgets for us after we had returned a pleasant message to the end user. This worked great. The user got a quick response from the server instead of having to wait 30 seconds for the widget to generate. There was, however, a small problem we neglected to mention: The widget-generation tasks were not being persisted. If the BackgroundDRb server crashed before it processed all the tasks, those tasks would be lost. For this situation, that might not be a problem, but what if we start to sell widgets? We can't take people's money if we never create their widgets.

Enter our new Amazing Widget product. The Amazing Widget slices, dices, juliennes, chops, and programs your DVR, all for the affordable price of only $19.99! Because we plan to start selling these new widgets, we want to make sure that in case of a problem we still can generate the widgets when the server starts working again. To do that, we need to start persisting our tasks.

First, let's set up our new Amazing Widgets. A quick little Rails scaffolding will get us most of the way to where we need to be:

```
$ ruby script/generate scaffold amazing_widget name:string body:
text price:decimal
```

Now we need to run our newly created migration so that we can build the amazing_widgets database table:

```
$ rake db:migrate
```

We also need to tweak our `AmazingWidget` class to be a subclass of the `Widget` class:

```
class AmazingWidget < Widget
  set_table_name 'amazing_widgets'

end
```

You'll notice that we have to tell ActiveRecord to use the `amazing_widgets` table via the `set_table_name` method. If we didn't do that, it would try to use the `widgets` table we created earlier.

With all that set up, we should be able to start our server, go to `http://localhost:3000/amazing_widgets/new`, and create a new Amazing Widget. If you did that, you would see that we have the same problem we had earlier—it takes 30 seconds to create a new Amazing Widget. That won't help us sell a lot of widgets, so let's place them in a queue and let BackgrounDRb handle it for us offline.

First, let's create a new worker to process these new widgets:

```
$ ruby script/generate worker amazing_widget
```

Now let's edit the file `lib/workers/amazing_widget_worker.rb` to do the processing we need:

```
class AmazingWidgetWorker < BackgrounDRb::MetaWorker

  set_worker_name :amazing_widget_worker

  def create(args = nil)
  end

  def create_new_widget(options = {})
    logger.debug "We need to create a new widget: #{options.inspect}"
    widget = AmazingWidget.create(options)
    # send an email here to let the customer know their
    # new Amazing Widget is ready!
    logger.debug "We created widget: #{options.inspect}"
    persistent_job.finish!
  end

end
```

As you can see, this is pretty much identical to the `WidgetWorker` class we created earlier.[5] In the `create_new_widget` method we create our new `AmazingWid-
get`. We also have a note in there about emailing the customer when the widget is
ready; you get that added perk for your $19.99. Finally, we call the `finish!` method
on the `persistent_job`[6] method. This call tells BackgrounDRb to mark the record
in the database as finished so that it doesn't again pull the task from the database and
attempt to run it.

With our `AmazingWidgetWorker` written, all we need to do is hook it up to our
controller, in much the same way we did with the `WidgetWorker` earlier. To do that,
let's rewrite the `create` action in `AmazingWidgetsController` to look like this:

```
def create
  widget_worker = MiddleMan.worker(:amazing_widget_worker)
  success = widget_worker.enq_create_new_widget(:arg =>
params[:amazing_widget], :job_key => params[:amazing_widget][:name])
  if success
    msg = 'We are creating your widget. Please check back shortly.'
    flash[:notice] = msg
    redirect_to(amazing_widgets_url)
  else
    @amazing_widget = AmazingWidget.new(params[:amazing_widget])
    msg = 'There was an error creating your widget. Please try again
          later.'
    flash[:error] = msg
    render(:action => 'new')
  end
end
```

Let's step through what is different this time around in comparison to our earlier
asynchronous version. Obviously, wherever we referenced `:widget_worker` or
`widget`, we need to replace it with `:amazing_widget_worker` or `amazing_
widget`. The biggest difference between persistent and asynchronous calls can be
found in this line:

```
success = widget_worker.enq_create_new_widget(:arg =>
 params[:amazing_widget], :job_key => params[:amazing_widget][:name])
```

When we wanted to call the `create_new_widget` method asynchronously, we
called it using the "magic" method `async_create_new_widget`. Now that we want

to use a persistent queue, we use the "magic" method `enq_create_new_widget`. The `enq` portion of the "magic" method tells BackgrounDRb to enqueue (put) the task into the persistent queue for processing.

In addition to the `:arg` parameter, which is a `Hash` containing the information we need to create a new `AmazingWidget`, we have to pass a unique `:job_key`. Here I am using the name of the widget as the `:job_key` parameter, but it can be anything you'd like, as long as it's unique.

It is worth pointing out that the `enq` "magic" method returns `true` or `false` depending on whether it can persist the record. This differs from the `async` "magic" method, which returns `ok` or `nil` depending on whether it was successful.

With everything in place, we can now request that BackgrounDRb create a new `AmazingWidget` offline using the `bdrb_job_queues` table to persist that request.

Before we start the BackgrounDRb server to handle these new tasks, let's create an `AmazingWidget` and briefly look at what the database entry looks like for our request. Start the Rails application and create a new `AmazingWidget`. Now, open your database in your favorite database viewer, and let's look at a few of the fields in our newly created record. The columns that are of importance to us are `worker_name`, `worker_method`, `job_key`, `started_at`, `finished_at`, and `args`:

- The `worker_name` column represents the name of the worker that is to be used for this task. In our case this value should be `amazing_widget_worker`. The `worker_method` column holds the name of the method we want to call on the aforementioned worker, so for us this value should be `create_new_widget`. The `job_key` column holds the unique identifier for the task. If you remember, earlier I used the name of the widget as the `job_key`, so the value I see in this column is `My Amazing Worker`.

- The `started_at` and `finished_at` columns should be fairly obvious. They tell you what time the task started processing and what time it finished. Right now these columns should both be `NULL`. Because we haven't started the BackgrounDRb server, the task has yet to start, so it cannot be finished. When we start our BackgrounDRb process and refresh this table, we see that these columns both get updated and that the difference between them should be just over 30 seconds, because our widgets take 30 seconds to build.

- The `args` column is an encrypted version of the arguments that we passed into the `enq_create_new_widget` method. This column is encrypted to protect the contents of the arguments, because they may contain sensitive data such as passwords, email addresses, or other such personal details.

Let's fire up our BackgrounDRb server:

```
$ ruby script/backgroundrb start
```

I also like to tail the log file so that I can see how things are progressing:

```
$ tail -f log/backgroundrb_11006.log
```

After a while we should see our log file spit out the following:

```
We need to create a new widget: {"price"=>"19.99", "name"=>
"My Amazing Widget", "body"=>"This is my new Amazing, and
 expensive, Widget!"}
We created widget: {"price"=>"19.99", "name"=>"My Amazing Widget",
 "body"=>"This is my new Amazing, and expensive, Widget!"}
```

If we refresh the row in the `bdrb_job_queues` table that represents the task we just processed, we see that it has been updated. My `started_at` column has the value `2009-07-19 22:52:26`, and the `finished_at` column has the value `2009-07-19 22:52:56`. As we predicted earlier, they are 30 seconds apart.

If you're observant, you will notice that a few other columns also got updated, including the `job_key` column. The value of my `job_key` column is now `finished_ 1248043976_My Amazing Widget`. BackgroundDRb updates this column and prepends the word "finished" as well as the timestamp of completion to the key we supplied. Because of this we now can reuse the `job_key`, should we so desire. This is useful if you have recurring tasks that happen periodically.

So with those few simple changes to the controller, and the generation of our new worker, we quickly got database persisted tasks working. Now we can feel confident when we go out and sell all those Amazing Widgets!

Caching Results with Memcached

As you've seen, offloading heavy and/or slow processes to BackgrounDRb can make your application a lot more useable and user-friendly. We can easily fire and forget these tasks and just let them complete in their own time. But how do we find out the current status of those tasks? What if we want to get the final result of some long-running calculation? What if we just want to let the user know via some fancy AJAX on the page when his or her widget has finished being generated? Well, BackgrounDRb has you covered.

BackgrounDRb supports the popular caching system Memcached.[7] Using Memcached we can easily place updates for and results of our tasks in the cache so that other services can come along, query, and take appropriate action based on what is in the cache.

Using the hooks to Memcached is easy. First we need to update our `back-groundrb.yml` file to tell BackgrounDRb where to find the Memcached servers:

```
---
:backgroundrb:
  :ip: 0.0.0.0
  :port: 11006

:memcache: "127.0.0.1:11211"
```

Just like earlier, when we discussed the `:client` configuration parameter, the `:memcache` parameter also accepts a comma-separated list of Memcached servers. In our example we are just running a single Memcached server on host 127.0.0.1:11211. This is all that is required to tell BackgrounDRb to use Memcached for its caching mechanism. If we do not specify this, BackgrounDRb uses its own internal caching scheme. This can prove problematic, so you should avoid it if you are planning on using caching.

With our application now configured to use Memcached, let's update our `AmazingWidgetWorker` class and put some information in there so that we can query it from the Rails console and see how our task is going. All we need to do is update the `create_new_widget` method in the `AmazingWidgetWorker` class:

```
def create_new_widget(options = {})
  cache[self.job_key] = "Generating... #{self.job_key}"
  widget = AmazingWidget.create(options)
  # send an email here to let the customer know their
  # new Amazing Widget is ready!
  cache[self.job_key] = "Completed... #{self.job_key}"
  persistent_job.finish!
end
```

I've replaced the logging statements we've previously had in the `create_new_widget` method with calls to the `cache` method. The `cache` method returns an instance of the `Memcache` class that holds a connection to the Memcached servers we configured earlier. The `Memcache` class presents itself much like the `Hash` class does. Because of this we can use the familiar `[]` syntax we are used to with a `Hash`.

Remember that earlier we had to create a unique `job_key` when we created a new task to be assigned to the `AmazingWidgetWorker`. Here we are using the unique `job_key` as the key with which we will store our messages in Memcached. Then we simply set two messages—one at the beginning of the process, stating that we are working on this task, and another at the end of the process, saying that we completed the process.

Earlier I mentioned updating the user via some fancy AJAX, but for our simple example we will just use the Rails console to find out the status of our widget task. I'll leave the building of that fancy AJAX to you, the reader, as a fun little add-on to this chapter. For now, let's see how this all works.

As we have been doing, fire up both the Rails server and the BackgrounDRb server so that we can create a new `AmazingWidget`. You also need to have a Memcached server running. This can easily be accomplished, assuming that you have Memcached installed, like this:

```
$ memcached -d
```

This runs an instance of Memcached in the background.

Finally, let's open an instance of the Rails console so that we can check the cache and find out how things are going:

```
$ ruby script/console
```

I know that this is a lot of different servers to start and get running, but trust me, it's definitely worth it. Go ahead and create a new `AmazingWidget` as we did earlier. Then go to the Rails console and run the following:

```
$ puts MiddleMan.worker(:amazing_widget_worker).ask_result('MC
Widget')
```

I created my new `AmazingWidget` with the name of "MC Widget," so that is also the `job_key`. Replace that as the parameter to the `ask_result` method if you created your `AmazingWidget` with a different name. We have not seen `ask_result` before.

Simply put, the `ask_result` method takes the key you used to store your messages into Memcached and then queries Memcached to get back the result.

Chances are, if you were quick enough, you probably got back `nil` from that statement. That is because BackgrounDRb had yet to start processing that task. Keep rerunning that command, and eventually you will see it start printing the following:

```
Generating... MC Widget
```

When you see that, you can wait 30 seconds and run it one last time. You should then see the following:

```
Completed... MC Widget
```

That's it! We quickly updated our application to allow BackgrounDRb to store results into Memcached. From there it was a stone's throw to actually using those results in our application.

Conclusion

BackgrounDRb is a very stable and mature library that has been around for quite a few years. This means that it has a good-sized installation base, a plethora of documentation, and plenty of quick support on the web. It allows you to easily offload your heavy and/or slow processing tasks to the background and move on, in a rather nice fire-and-forget sort of way.

Like most DRb-based libraries, BackgrounDRb suffers from a scalability problem: DRb, as a whole, quickly becomes too cumbersome, slow, and unstable when you start to outgrow a small installation.[8] This means that using the clustering aspects of BackgrounDRb, while cool, could prove to be more trouble than it's worth. What I might recommend is maintaining a one-to-one ratio of application servers to BackgrounDRb servers. This means having a dedicated BackgrounDRb server for each of your servers. That way you don't have to try and send a lot of data across the wire, and things should scale a little better.

Overall, BackgrounDRb is strong and reliable. It has some quirks, and there are times when I wish a few different architectural choices had been made. As a side note, having to type BackgrounDRb this many times has nearly driven me crazy. Be thankful that you have to type it only a few times when you are actually using the library!

As you will see in the next chapter, there are alternatives to BackgrounDRb, so be sure to explore them as well.

Endnotes

1. http://backgroundrb.rubyforge.org/

2. http://gnufied.org/

3. http://github.com/collectiveidea/delayed_job/tree/master, http://www.hoptoadapp.com/. Also see Chapter 10, "Delayed Job."

4. http://en.wikipedia.org/wiki/Round-robin_scheduling

5. Obviously if this were a real-world application, I would have cleaned up all the redundancies between `Widget` and `AmazingWidget`. But for the sake of these examples, it's just easier to demonstrate them as separate classes and systems.

6. This is what the documentation on BackgrounDRb has to say about the `persistent_job` method: "persistent_job is a thread local variable and will refer to currently running queued task can be used from thread pool as well." To clarify this point, this call is thread-safe.

7. http://www.danga.com/memcached/. Also see Chapter 6, "Politics."

8. Your mileage may vary, but for me, after about 20 servers, things can start getting pretty hairy as far as `DRb` services are concerned.

CHAPTER 10

Delayed Job

This book has covered many different ways to handle background tasks. We have talked about using distributed messaging queues, such as RabbitMQ and Starling. We have discussed using token workers, such as Politics, to process those queues. We also have talked about using background servers, such as BackgrounDRb, to hand off those tasks so that they can be processed. All these approaches have their advantages and disadvantages. Some offer higher performance, some offer greater redundancy, and some offer simple interfaces.

In February 2008, Tobias Lütke[1] announced the release of the Delayed Job[2] plugin. This plugin was extracted from the Shopify[3] project he works on. Tobias wrote Delayed Job with the idea that it would combine the best parts of these other systems while trying to leave out the bad parts.[4]

The idea behind Delayed Job is simple: Send the task you want to be performed in the background to the queue. In the case of Delayed Job, the queue is database backed. Then start a background process that pops tasks off the queue, locks them, and tries to process them. When the task is finished, it is marked as complete. If there is a problem, the error is recorded, and the task is tried again. Sounds simple, right? Well, let's dive in and see if that is in fact the case.

Installation

I made the following disclaimer in the preceding chapter, but I feel it would be wise to repeat it:

Before we jump into installing and configuring Delayed Job, let me state that I'm assuming you are already familiar with Ruby on Rails, its structure and layout, what a Rails plugin is, and other such generalities.

Now, with the formalities out of the way, let's get going. First, let's create our new Rails project:

```
$ rails djob
```

With our Rails project created, we can install Delayed Job. Unlike BackgrounDRb, Delayed Job has no prerequisite gems that need to be installed. So installing the plugin is simply a matter of running the following command from within the Rails application folder:

```
$ ruby script/plugin install
 git://github.com/collectiveidea/delayed_job.git
```

I would like to take this opportunity to point out that the URL we used to install the plugin is actually a fork of the original project. Currently this fork is generally considered to be the best version of Delayed Job. As you will see in a minute, it has a few enhanced offerings, including a generator to generate the necessary migrations and files we need. This may change in the future. Should you want to use Tobias's original version of the project, or if he merges in the changes from other forks, you can find the original version at http://github.com/tobi/delayed_job/tree/master.

As I mentioned, we need to generate a migration to create the table that Delayed Job will use to store the tasks you ask it to perform. To do that we can use the built-in generator to create the migration:

```
$ ruby script/generate delayed_job
```

This should generate the following migration:

```
class CreateDelayedJobs < ActiveRecord::Migration
  def self.up
    create_table :delayed_jobs, :force => true do |table|
      table.integer  :priority, :default => 0
      table.integer  :attempts, :default => 0
      table.text     :handler
      table.text     :last_error
      table.datetime :run_at
      table.datetime :locked_at
```

```
      table.datetime :failed_at
      table.string   :locked_by
      table.timestamps
    end

  end

  def self.down
    drop_table :delayed_jobs
  end
end
```

As you can see, the `delayed_jobs` table is actually very simple and straightforward. We will look at some of these columns in a bit more detail later in this chapter. I suspect that most columns will be pretty self-explanatory, because they are well named.

With the migration generated, let's run it so that we can add the table to the database:

```
$ rake db:migrate
```

That's it. Delayed Job is now installed and ready to accept tasks from our application.

Sending It Later with Delayed Job

One day you are in the shower when you have a brainstorm for what will be the next "killer" web app. Wouldn't it be great if there were a website where people could upload their videos and share them with the rest of the world? How could it fail? It's a great idea, and no one else has done it before.

You rush to the phone, soaking wet and with shampoo still in your hair, and call me about your great idea. I rush right over to help with the coding. Later that afternoon, after I insist that you put on some clothes, we launch the beta site, and the visitors start to pour in. There's a problem, though. When people upload their videos, it can take up to a minute for the server to encode them into the proper video format for use with the site. The visitors are quickly leaving the site because they don't want to wait that long. What should we do?

Delayed Job can come to the rescue. Let's take a look at how it can help solve our video encoding problem.

So what does our code look like right now? Well, first we created our `Video` class with the following command:

```
$ ruby script/generate scaffold video title:string
 description:text file_name:string encoded:Boolean
```

That created our migration, controller, and model classes. Next we updated our `Video` class to add a method to do the encoding. So now our `Video` class looks like this:

```
class Video < ActiveRecord::Base

  def encode
    logger.info "Encoding #{self.file_name}..."
    sleep(rand(60))
    self.encoded = true
    self.save!
    logger.info "Finished encoding #{self.file_name}."
  end

end
```

As you can see, the `encode` method can take up to 60 seconds to complete. That's a long time to expect our visitors to wait for the page to return to them. Let's look at what the `create` action on our `VideosController` looks like:

```
def create
  @video = Video.new(params[:video])
  if @video.save
    @video.encode
    flash[:notice] = 'Video was successfully created.'
    redirect_to(@video)
  else
    render :action => "new"
  end
end
```

After we successfully save the new video, we call the `encode` method, and the user is forced to sit and wait until it is finished.

So how can we use Delayed Job to fix this? The answer is surprisingly easy. We just need to invoke the `send_later` method. Let's see what our `create` action looks like when we call the `send_later` method, and then we'll talk about what it does and where it comes from:

```
def create
  @video = Video.new(params[:video])
  if @video.save
    @video.send_later(:encode)
    msg = 'Video was successfully created.'
    msg << "\nIt is being encoded and will be available shortly."
    flash[:notice] = msg
    redirect_to(@video)
  else
    render :action => "new"
  end
end
```

All we did was replace the call to the `encode` method with a call to the `send_later` method, passing in `:encode` as the argument to the method. The `send_later` method works pretty much like the `send` method does in Ruby, with one big difference. When you call the `send` method in Ruby, you pass it the name of the method you want to execute, and the `send` method then executes that method. The `send_later` method also expects you to pass in the name of the method you want to execute. In our case we pass in `:encode`, but it does not execute the method. Instead, the `send_later` method actually creates a new task in the `delayed_jobs` table, with a message saying that the `encode` method should be executed when the task is run.

Now when we use our Rails application to create a new video, we see that the server very quickly responds with our new flash message telling the user that his or her video is being encoded and will be available shortly. If we looked in the database, we would see that there is now a task sitting in the `delayed_jobs` table. We should also see that the `encoded` column on our new video record is set to `false` because it has not yet been encoded.

So how do we process our new task? There are two ways to process tasks. The first is recommended for development purposes because it runs in the foreground and provides simple debugging:

```
$ rake jobs:work
```

In production it is recommended that you use the following code, because it automatically daemonizes:

```
$ ruby script/delayed_job start -e production
```

The `delayed_job` script is another reason why you should use the aforementioned fork of Delayed Job. That script is not in the original project, and it comes in handy when you're trying to start a daemonized instance of the process.

> ## Help with script/delayed_job Parameters
>
> `script/delayed_job` has a handful of useful parameters that can be passed in when starting/stopping it. Rather unfortunately, it also has two different ways to find out what those parameters are.
>
> The first way is to simply call the script without any parameters:
>
> ```
> $ ruby script/delayed_job
> ```
>
> Under the covers the script uses the Daemons[5] gem to wrap itself with start/stop/restart commands. Calling the script without any parameters gives you a printout of what the Daemons gem expects for parameters.
>
> The second way to find out what parameters are available is with the following:
>
> ```
> $ ruby script/delayed_job --help
> ```
>
> This prints the parameters that Delayed Job allows you to pass in that affect its operations. For example:
>
> ```
> Usage: delayed_job [options] start|stop|restart|run
>   -h, --help                    Show this
>                                 message
>   -e, --environment=NAME        Specifies the
>                                 environment to
> ```

```
                                          run jobs
                                          under (test/
                                          development/
                                          production).
          --min-priority N                Minimum priority
                                          of jobs to run.
          --max-priority N                Maximum priority
                                          of jobs to run.
   -n, --number_of_workers=workers        Number of unique
                                          workers to spawn
```

Running the command both ways provides you with a
good understanding of how to configure the script to meet
your needs.

For our examples, let's use the Rake task, because it provides some helpful output.

With the Rake task running, we just need to wait up to 60 seconds before we see
that our task has been processed. When it is processed, we should see something similar to the following:

```
*** Starting job worker host:macbates.home pid:22858
1 jobs processed at 0.0240 j/s, 0 failed ...
```

To verify that it actually worked, we can look at the `encoded` column for our video
record and see that it is now set to `true`.

Unlimited Processing—Kind Of

A couple of problems are commonly a source of frustration
with other background task processing systems. Those
problems are that they usually require another running
server, or you can fire up only one processing task on each
machine, or you can fire up as many processors you want.
But they all invoke the Rails environment, causing a lot of
memory and CPU to be consumed, and they do it each
time the processor fires up.

> These exact problems are what led the site GitHub.com[6] to
> start using Delayed Job.
>
> Delayed Job, whether you are using the Rake task or the
> bundled script, allows you to start as many instances as you
> want, on as many boxes as you want. These instances then
> run forever using an infinite loop. This means that Delayed
> Job loads the Rails environment only once and does not
> keep starting it each time the process kicks off. This makes
> for a very efficient use of system resources.
>
> Delayed Job also offers sophisticated locking mechanisms
> to help ensure that tasks are processed by multiple proces-
> sors at the same time.

Custom Workers and Delayed Job

As you just saw, the `send_later` method makes it incredibly easy to use Delayed Job.
But what happens if we want to perform something more complicated than just calling a method on a class? For example, let's look at the great video website we've built.
Our site uses QuickTime for its video codec, so do we need to waste precious resources
re-encoding a video that is already in the correct format? I don't think so. We need to
encode only those pesky .wma Windows files that people upload.

To solve this problem, we have two choices. We could change our `encode`
method in the `Video` class to look like this:

```
def encode
  if File.extname(self.file_name) == '.wma'
    logger.info "Encoding #{self.file_name}..."
    sleep(rand(60))
    self.encoded = true
    self.save!
    logger.info "Finished encoding #{self.file_name}."
  else
    self.encoded = true
    self.save!
  end
end
```

That works. But now we've cluttered up our model with crazy logic determining whether we should actually perform the encoding. So what are the alternatives?

Well, Delayed Job allows you to create custom worker classes that can be added to the queue. Delayed Job requires that your class fulfill a simple interface. You just need to make sure that your class has a `perform` method on it. That's it. Really. Just a `perform` method. You don't need to include any modules or extend any classes.

Let's see what our custom `VideoWorker` class would look like:

```ruby
class VideoWorker

  attr_accessor :video_id

  def initialize(video_id)
    self.video_id = video_id
  end

  def perform
    video = Video.find(video_id, :conditions => {:encoded => false})
    if video
      if File.extname(video.file_name) == '.wma'
        video.encode
      else
        video.encoded = true
        video.save!
      end
    end
  end

end
```

As you can see, we have a plain old Ruby class called `VideoWorker`. This class has an accessor called `video_id`. This will be the `id` of the video we want to work on. We have an `initialize` method that lets us set the `video_id` attribute. Finally, we have our `perform` method. The `perform` method finds the correct, unencoded video. If it exists, the method checks to see if the format is a Windows Media file. If it is, `perform` calls the `encode` method. If not, it marks the video as encoded, saves it, and then finishes.

Now that we have our custom `VideoWorker`, how do we use it to create a new task for Delayed Job to perform? Well, let's take another look at our `create` action in `VideosController` and see how it changes:

```
def create
  @video = Video.new(params[:video])
  if @video.save
    Delayed::Job.enqueue(VideoWorker.new(@video.id))
    msg = 'Video was successfully created.'
    msg << "\nIt is being encoded and will be available shortly."
    flash[:notice] = msg
    redirect_to(@video)
  else
    render :action => "new"
  end
end
```

We replaced the line that called the send_later method with the following:

```
Delayed::Job.enqueue(VideoWorker.new(@video.id))
```

We create a new instance of the VideoWorker class we just built and pass it in the id of the video object. We then call the enqueue method on the Delayed::Job class and pass it the VideoWorker instance we just created. That then creates the task for us in the database. Again, that's all there is to it. When the Delayed Job process runs, it executes the perform method on our instance of the VideoWorker class we created, just the same as if we had used send_later instead.

> **Easy Workers, and a Few Extra Little Helpers**
>
> While writing this book I became enamored with Delayed Job, and I have started to use it on pretty much every project. In doing so, I have collected a handful of useful little extras into a gem, delayed_job_extras, which can be found at http://github.com/markbates/delayed_job_extras/ tree.
>
> So what are these extras? Well, there is support for Hoptoad notifications. This means that instead of just sticking an exception in the database, Delayed Job will also send a message to your Hoptoad account so that you can track the error.

There is support for the `is_paranoid` gem. This will "soft" delete jobs after they have been processed. The benefit of this is reporting.

Which brings us to…the `stats` method on `Delayed::Job`. This will tell you things such has the total jobs in the system (by worker), the number of remaining jobs, the number of processed jobs, and the number of failed jobs.

Finally, it also gives you a base worker class, `Delayed::Worker`, which you can implement for your custom workers. This will properly handle Hoptoad notifications, should you use them, so you don't have to. It also gives you a `logger` method so you have easy access to the `RAILS_DEFAULT_LOGGER` constant.

The `Delayed::Worker` class also helps you to DRY up your code. Quickly looking at our `VideoWorker`, we would rewrite it to look like the following using `Delayed::Worker`:

```
class VideoWorker < Delayed::Worker

  attr_accessor :video_id

  def initialize(video_id)
    self.video_id = video_id
  end

  perform do
    video = Video.find(video_id, :conditions =>
{:encoded => false})
    if video
      if File.extname(video.file_name) == '.wma'
        video.encode
      else
        video.encoded = true
        video.save!
      end
```

```
      end
    end

end
```

It doesn't look like we changed much—in fact, we didn't. We made `VideoWorker` a subclass of `Delayed::Worker` and we changed the method definition of `perform` to use a class level method named `perform` and pass it a block. With those few changes, however, we now have Hoptoad support, we can now search through our `delayed_jobs` table for jobs for this specific worker, and we can change our code to create a new job from this:

```
Delayed::Job.enqueue(VideoWorker.new(1))
```

To this:

```
VideoWorker.enqueue(1)
```

That is much more readable!

There are a few more tricks up this gem's sleeve, but I'll let you dig into them a bit more, should you want to.

It's Just ActiveRecord

The `Delayed::Job` class is just a souped-up `Active Record::Base` class. That means we just use it to query the `delayed_jobs` table, just like any other `Active Record::Base` class.

For example, from inside the Rails Console we can make a call like the following:

```
$ puts Delayed::Job.first.inspect
```

And we should expect to see something like the following returned:

```
#<Delayed::Job id: 21, priority: 0, attempts: 0,
 handler: "--- !ruby/object:VideoWorker \nvideo_id:
 23\n", last_error: nil, run_at: "2009-07-27
 01:34:50", locked_at: nil, failed_at: nil,
 locked_by: nil, created_at: "2009-07-27 01:34:50",
 updated_at: "2009-07-27 01:34:50">
```

Now you can use the `Delayed::Job` class to build your own processor to run reports with, or anything else your heart desires.

Here is where I let you in on a little secret: The `send_later` method creates an instance of a class called `Delayed::PerformableMethod`. It passes the method you want to call and the current object's information to this class. Then it calls the `enqueue` method on the `Delayed::Job` class, passing it the instance of `Delayed::PerformableMethod`, just like we did earlier. Now you know Delayed Job's `send_later` dirty little secret.

Who's on First, and When Does He Steal Second?

When you're creating tasks in any large system, sometimes the issue arises of which tasks to process first and when certain tasks are supposed to run. Delayed Job has a simple system in place to help you schedule and prioritize your tasks.

Suppose our video site has become the largest and most popular video site on the web.[7] Because we are the biggest and best, we will offer our users a premium service. The most exciting perk that comes with this service is that the user's videos are encoded before videos from users who don't pay for the service. We might also want to place the encoding of certain members' videos even higher in the queue if they have enough positive ratings, or followers, or some other very Web 2.0/social networking type of qualification.

So how do we place such a video higher in the queue? We assign it a priority number. So far, whenever we have created a new task in the queue, it has been given a priority level of 0. All we need to do is pass a second argument to either the `send_later` method or the `enqueue` method. They both take the same arguments, so all the following examples apply to both.

To place a video higher in the queue, we just need to do the following:

```
@video.send_later(:encode, 1)
```

Because 1 is greater than 0, Delayed Job processes this video first. When Delayed Job goes to fetch tasks from the delayed_jobs table, it appends the following to the SQL it generates:

```
priority DESC, run_at ASC
```

It first sorts on the priority column, with records of the highest priorities first in the list. It then sorts by the run_at column, getting the oldest records first (but we'll get to that in a minute).

Because the priority column is just an Integer, we can use both positive and negative numbers when assigning priority. For example, our paid premium members get a priority of greater than 0, our nonpaid members get a priority of 0, and our unverified new users get a priority of less than 0.

As you just saw, the run_at column does just what its name suggests: It allows us to tell Delayed Job when we want to run a particular task. For example, we want to create a task for each of our users that charges their credit cards on the first of each month. We also want to make sure that those tasks get a very high priority, because they're the most important to the business. To do that, we might create a custom worker like the following. (Please note that unless you've actually created all the code to back all of this, the following examples are just for show, not for running.)

```
class PaymentWorker

  attr_accessor :user_id

  def initialize(user_id)
    self.user_id = user_id
  end

  def perform
    user = User.find(user_id)
    payment_info = user.payment_info
    if payment_info.charge(19.99)
```

```
        Postman.deliver_payment_charged_email(user)
        Delayed::Job.enqueue(PaymentWorker.new(user_id),
                             1000,
                             1.month.from_now.beginning_of_month)
      else
        Postman.deliver_payment_failure_email(user)
        Delayed::Job.enqueue(PaymentWorker.new(user_id),
                             2000,
                             1.day.from_now)
      end
    end

  end
```

When the user signs up for the premium service, we would add a task to the system that charges her credit card immediately, with a high priority, such as this:

```
Delayed::Job.enqueue(PaymentWorker.new(@user.id), 1000)
```

We give our task a priority of 1000, ensuring that it gets attention pretty quickly. In our `PaymentWorker` we find the user and attempt to charge her credit card. If we succeed, we create another task with a high priority of 1000 and set it to run at the beginning of the next month. Then we send the customer an email letting her know we charged her account. Should the payment fail, we send the customer an email letting her know that it failed, and we add another task that tries again the following day to charge her account. But this time we make it even a higher priority to ensure that it gets first attention.

You can rest assured that Delayed Job is smart enough to not run your task until its time has come. With that said, Delayed Job makes no guarantees that it will run your task at the precise time you set it to be run. The column `run_at` is slightly misnamed. It really should be named `run_after_at`.

Configuring Delayed Job

Normally a section on configuring a library would be at the beginning of the chapter. I just felt that to help you understand the relatively few configuration settings that Delayed Job offers, it would help to understand what Delayed Job does and how it works.

To set our configuration settings, we would create an initializer file, delayed_job.rb, in the config/initializers directory, that looks like this:

```
Delayed::Job.destroy_failed_jobs = false

silence_warnings do
  Delayed::Job.const_set("MAX_ATTEMPTS", 3)
  Delayed::Job.const_set("MAX_RUN_TIME", 5.minutes)
end
```

So what do these settings mean, and what are their defaults? Let's start with the first one:

```
Delayed::Job.destroy_failed_jobs = false
```

By default, if a task continues to fail and has hit the maximum number of attempts allotted, Delayed Job purges (read deletes) those tasks from the database. The downside of this, as you can imagine, is that unless you are paying close attention to what is happening with your tasks, it is possible that you will lose important information about what is causing these errors and how to fix them. By setting destroy_failed_jobs to false, you are telling Delayed Job to keep these tasks around, and not delete them, but to stop attempting to process them. The only downside of this approach is that you can start to clutter up your delayed_jobs table with failed tasks. However, I still recommend that you always set this to false.

As we just talked about, Delayed Job attempts to process a task for a set number of tries before it fails and finally declares the task a lost cause. The default setting for this is 25. You can change this setting like this:

```
Delayed::Job.const_set("MAX_ATTEMPTS", 3)
```

Delayed Job also uses the MAX_ATTEMPTS variable to determine the wait between each attempt at the task. The algorithm for setting the next run_at date is as follows:

```
Time.now + (attempt ** 4) + 5
```

If the attempt variable were the maximum default of 25, that would result in a date that is 100 hours into the future. This means that it would take a full 20 days between when the task first runs and when it has failed for the last time. The reason for this ever-increasing span of time is that it is assumed that as time passes, it is less and less likely that the task will succeed, so why keep pounding the system with it?

Finally, we can set a task's expected maximum length as follows:

```
Delayed::Job.const_set("MAX_RUN_TIME", 5.minutes)
```

The default for MAX_RUN_TIME is 4 hours. This should be set to the amount of time you think your longest task will take. If a task exceeds this time, it is possible that another process can pick it up and start to work on it, so keep that in mind when defining this parameter.

I would like to share another configuration setting with you. This one is a bit different from the others, because it doesn't necessarily configure Delayed Job. Rather, it helps you configure your code. I know that statement doesn't make much sense, but please bear with me.

In one of your environments, such as production.rb, you can place the following code:

```
config.after_initialize do
  Video.handle_asynchronously :encode
end
```

This performs a bit of "magic" under the covers. It creates an alias of the encode method we created on the Video class and sets it up to create a new task whenever you call it. For example, now if we call the following code:

```
@video.encode
```

it is the equivalent of calling this code:

```
@video.send_later(:encode)
```

The advantage is that we don't have to update our code all over the place, because all calls to the encode method now generate tasks to be run later.

As you can imagine, this is a really cool feature. Unfortunately, I've never quite been able to make it work. I've tried it on numerous projects and on various types of classes, and I've never had any luck with it. I mention it because others don't seem to have any problems with it. I hope by the time you read this I too can use this awesome feature. Try it for yourself and see if it works for you.

> **Deploying Delayed Job**
>
> Be sure to check out the recipes folder that is included with the Delayed Job plugin. Inside you will find a complete Capistrano[8] recipe that starts, stops, and restarts the background processes for you when you deploy your application.
>
> This is a great time to point out that it is *very* important that you restart your Delayed Job processes when you do a deployment. Those processes will still be executing on your old code base, not the new one. This can cause serious errors and headaches when you're trying to debug the problem. Trust me. I'm speaking from experience.

Conclusion

You have seen how Delayed Job is easy to integrate into our application and provides several flexible, easy-to-use ways of interacting with it. It comes full-featured out of the box, without any dependencies[9] and very little configuration. Its simplicity means that you can easily integrate it into your application and that you have no excuse for not offloading those heavy tasks to a background process.

Despite its benefits, you still need to keep in mind a few issues when using Delayed Job. For a start, because it is database-backed, you still have the added overhead of creating a new ActiveRecord object and persisting it to the database when you create a new task. That's a decent amount of overhead that shouldn't be discounted, especially if the task you are offloading is just creating a record in the database.

Delayed Job should be used for slow tasks that can be performed offline, as well as tasks that may rely on external services that may go down. A good example of this is sending emails. Because it's possible that the gateway might be down, it would be nice to have a reliable way of resending those emails later.

Like all the other technologies described in this book, using Delayed Job has pros and cons. You just have to ask yourself if the pros are the right pros for you, and if you can live with the cons.

Endnotes

1. http://blog.leetsoft.com/

2. http://github.com/tobi/delayed_job/tree/master

3. http://www.shopify.com/

4. Of course, isn't that what everyone tries to do when writing a library?

5. http://daemons.rubyforge.org/

6. http://github.com/blog/197-the-new-queue

7. Of course, we know this won't actually happen unless we allow adult content. I'm not saying we should; I'm just saying we could probably make a lot of money if we did.

8. http://www.capify.org

9. This is actually a little white lie. If you want to use the `delayed_job` script to start the process, you need to have the `daemons` gem installed for it to work. However, Delayed Job as a library requires no dependencies to work if you use the built-in Rake task.

Index

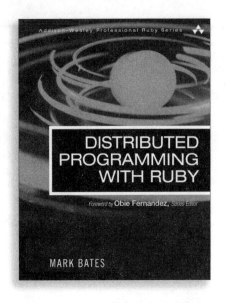

Your purchase of *Distributed Programming with Ruby* includes access to a free online edition for 45 days through the Safari Books Online subscription service. Nearly every Addison-Wesley Professional book is available online through Safari Books Online, along with more than 5,000 other technical books and videos from publishers such as Cisco Press, Exam Cram, IBM Press, O'Reilly, Prentice Hall, Que, and Sams.

SAFARI BOOKS ONLINE allows you to search for a specific answer, cut and paste code, download chapters, and stay current with emerging technologies.

Activate your FREE Online Edition at
www.informit.com/safarifree

> **STEP 1:** Enter the coupon code: FTIQFDB.

> **STEP 2:** New Safari users, complete the brief registration form.
> Safari subscribers, just log in.

If you have difficulty registering on Safari or accessing the online edition, please e-mail customer-service@safaribooksonline.com